How to
(Really)
Make Money
Blogging

How to (Really) Make Money Blogging

Cherie Burbach

Bonjour Publishing

How to (Really) Make Money Blogging

Bonjour Publishing

How to (Really) Make Money Blogging/ Cherie Burbach. —1st ed.
ISBN 978-0-9834750-9-5

Also by Cherie Burbach

Nonfiction

Creative Day Planner

21 Simple Things You Can Do To Help Someone With Diabetes

Internet Dating Is Not Like Ordering a Pizza

21 Ways to Promote Your Book on Twitter

Poetry

My Soul Is From a Different Place

Father's Eyes

The Difference Now

A New Dish

New and Selected Poems

Yes, You

For all the writers
who seek to inspire, inform, and create

Table of Contents

"To blog or not to blog… that is the question."

~ Cherie Burbach

Blogging for a Living

Where Are You In Your Writing Career?

People get into blogging for different reasons. Some are trying to make a full-time living as a writer. Others just want a few extra bucks or to add strength to their brand. Many authors blog to help sell their books but also want to earn money to provide for the time in between advances or sales. Others blog to express themselves or to teach.

The emergence of indie authors, who may write for traditional publishers but also publish books independently, has helped blogging become even more popular. It's a way to connect with readers as well as maintain a writing career.

No matter where you are in your writing journey, blogging can help you reach your goals. I centered this book on making a full or part-time income as a blogger, but the truth is blogging can benefit you indirectly through referrals and brand building as well, which also helps drive sales. Whether you are a seasoned freelance writer or budding novelist, you can use blogging for a variety of purposes that all benefit your income.

My Story

I've been a full-time blogger for a decade, writing for places like About.com, NBC/Universal, *Christianity Today* and Match.com. I also own and operate several of my own blogs, which help with income and keep my brand solid. But I got into blogging almost by accident. In 2005, I had written a book about Internet dating and was trying to figure out how to market it. I based the book on the approach I took when it came to online dating. I met over 60 guys for coffee in just six months, one of whom turned out to be the man I would marry just a year later.

I discovered that there are two things people commonly say to you when you tell them about your experience. One is: You should write a book. That's exactly what people said when they heard my story. (The other thing people say is: You're writing that? So-and-so already wrote a book like that!)

People are going to project their own preferences on you, but you have to write the kind of books you want to write for your own reasons. I decided to write and publish a book, *At the Coffee Shop*, as a way to encourage people to try online dating. I outlined my own experience and the method I had taken in setting up dates, writing my profile, and meeting new people. For me, online dating was a positive experience. Since so many people (at least the ones I had personally talked to) seemed to have such a negative attitude with online dating I wanted to be a source of inspiration for them.

The Beginning of Content Marketing

I had read somewhere that writing articles for free and giving them to websites in exchange for a link to your book was good practice. This was an early form of blogging for me and I began to study SEO, which in 2005 was a completely new term (at least to me!). Up until then, I had written freelance articles on the side while still working full-time. Occasionally, some of those articles were also posted online, but I quickly found out that blogging was different than just posting things to a website. There was a method to it, a purpose. It seemed to pair well with things like Facebook and Twitter. The more you did it, the more bloggers you met and the better you got at not just writing for yourself, but for the people who would take the time to read your stuff.

Sending all those articles to websites in order to promote my dating book was content marketing, although I didn't know it then. In learning how people read online, I began to format articles differently. The more I read about the philosophy of writing online, the more I adapted what I'd learned in order to broaden my skillset as a blogger.

When my dating book came out, I was also trying to start up a freelance writing business. I wrote for several publications, mainly from applying for job ads. Applying for jobs this way isn't terrible, but I've since learned that it wasn't the best way, either. I'll highlight more about where to find great gigs that pay you real money later on.

My dating book was the beginning of a writing career for me. Someone bought my book off of Amazon and contacted me about working for his site. He ran a website that had quasi celebrity writers who all wrote about dating, and online daters would hire them to write and improve their Internet dating profiles. He liked my writing style and thought it would fit in well with his site.

As I looked at his website, however, I had doubts. There was someone who edited a popular men's magazine, a couple of hip, fun young women who talked about dating in New York, a national radio show host, and a couple well-known authors that had written books. These were people much more popular than me in the dating world. Who would want to work with me, I wondered.

But that was exactly what made me stand out on this site. I was one of the few people who had tried online dating and met someone special that way. What's more, I felt online daters were brave. They put themselves out there and that was inspiring to me.

I worked as a dating consultant for about three years. I loved it. In this time I continued to write articles about dating and relationships, but instead of sending them to places for free I was now getting paid. This was the beginning of my writing career, and it all started because of blogging, but I didn't realize it then.

What's Your Brand?

Very often when you start a writing career, you're asked what makes you different than someone else. In other words, "Why should we hire you?" or "Why is your book different?" Knowing your brand, or what you represent, is extremely helpful in answering this question.

When I wrote for that online profile website, I instantly saw what made me different than other writers, and this was part of my brand. I wanted to genuinely help people and believed that all the questions people had were smart ones. I didn't look down at people that came to me for help because I admired their courage in stepping out into something unknown and trying to improve their lives. Oh, and I was one of "those people," who took a chance to change her life and succeeded.

I also wasn't the coolest kid on the block, the well-known celebrity, or the person who worked with daters just to get topics for a radio show. I had been through some things in life, and this helped me understand the issues readers ask me about. Even now, I think my brand is about helping people connect and encouraging them to be the person they were meant to be, whether it's nonfiction, fiction, or poetry.

Knowing your brand is tremendously helpful as a writer. You'll be asked what makes you different plenty of times when you're pitching a story, trying to get your fiction published, or getting your blog to stand out. You might know exactly what your brand is right now, but if you don't, it will come to you. A brand is different than something like a tagline, although the two can be related. Sometimes your readers and even the editors that hire you will have a better idea of what your brand is than you do. It's the overall vibe someone gets when reading your work. It's what they know they can expect from you.

Once I knew what my brand stood for, it made applying for jobs much easier. I got hired for that online dating profile site because of my brand, even before I knew what it was.

Why I Like Writing Online

When I first started out in freelancing, I did a variety of work both online and in print. Now, I write primarily online, and I love it. Focusing on the online world helped me specialize as a blogger. I have stayed current with trends with search, how people read online, and what types of questions readers want answered. This helps me tailor my writing to what people most want to read.

You can do the same thing. Whatever your area of expertise, you can either reach out to your existing audience or find new people to connect with. In the process, you'll also be strengthening your platform and attracting fans. Here's why I like writing primarily for the Internet.

Not as Much Pitching

Pitching ideas to editors is part of the job as a freelancer, but with blogging you get right down to writing and don't spend as much on the pitch. This is true whether you're writing for yourself or (as I'll cover later in this book) when you're trying to get hired as a regular freelancer. Regular work and establishing long-term relationships with clients will help you get right to work instead of talking about what to write. This will help you make more money, because time is money. Never underestimate the value of getting right to a project.

I used to waste a lot of time pitching ideas, waiting, and then when I finally got the go-ahead it seemed like I'd have to rush and get it done (because we'd spent so much time talking about it.) It wasn't my thing.

With blogging, I work on developing relationships with clients. Rather than just pitching one idea or blog post, I try to get an agreement to blog for several months. This is not only more efficient for me as a writer, but it also helps the client. Blogging is a little like exercise. If you do one post it's good, but you won't reap the long-term benefits until you do it regularly. Showing clients that regular blogging is beneficial to their website is a good way to get repeat business.

When you're a regular blogger for someone, they typically want you to come up with the topics and will give you the freedom to choose them. This means you're writing about the things that you want rather than asking permission to write about them and waiting for a response.

Freedom to Choose Article Subject Matter

For most of my clients I have a topic area to cover but coming up with the articles is my responsibility. I like the freedom this gives me. It allows me to further connect with readers and build on the articles they most visit and comment on.

Allowing me to be creative in blogging helps me come up with original ideas. Don't you find that much of the Internet is the same story repeated over and over by different "news outlets" or websites? If you're at the top of your game as a blogger, you don't do this. Instead, you take a subject and find a new way to cover it. This approach helps me be more creative in other areas I write in as well, and keeps my job fresh and fun.

Getting Paid

One thing that I find a total drag about running a business is chasing down clients for money. I have had far less problems (really, almost none) with my online clients. My offline clients require more work for billing even when they are on time with payments.

In addition, if you can secure a couple longer term contracts, you can usually count on a certain amount of money at a specific point each month, which makes bill paying and income planning so many easier. Part of the reason freelance writing is such a scary business to manage is because it is very up and down. But one way to combat that is by getting regular clients you know will pay you either by direct deposit or PayPal. Both of these make it easier to collect the money you're owed.

When I started out freelancing, I knew I had to make a certain amount of money in order to pay the bills. This was my goal, and goal setting is very important in writing. This will help you choose the right clients and also help you stay on track with where you want to go in your career.

Full or Part Time Income

One of the most common questions I get asked is if it's possible to make a full-time living as a blogger. It is, but it's like any small business. In order to make a full-time (livable) wage from blogging, you need to put in full-time (plus!) hours, just as you would if you were running any other type of small business. This period of long hours and intense work won't last forever, but in the beginning you will probably be logging in the hours in order to develop a comfort level with writing full-time. It's more than just sitting at a computer. It includes running your business, finding clients, billing, advertising, and keeping up on trends and technology. The writing might even seem secondary to everything else you're doing at first.

I write full-time now but started out part-time. I kept a part-time job for a while as I built up my client base. This gave me the security of having some money coming in while I searched for new work.

But even with that, I worked almost full-time to build clients and establish my business. It is possible to make a living from writing online. Or, if a writer has other income (from ebooks, classes, speaking engagements, or even a part-time job), writing online can be a good way to make money part-time.

Many writers assume blogging will bring them a full-time income if they only do it part-time. While that could happen, it's best to look at blogging the same as you would any other entrepreneurial venture. The more you put into it, the more you'll get out of it, including money.

Flexible, Work-From-Home Schedule

When I say "I work full time" what I mean is that I have work that equates to a full time schedule. However, even with that I still have flexibility. I can write at night or on weekends if I want to. I can post ahead and then use the rest of the time in the month to work on my novels, attend a lunch meeting, or run errands. I like being able to schedule my time this way.

Some writers I know are novelists who pen a couple books a year. Blogging helps them even out their income and the flexibility allows them to have some money coming in while they work on their books.

I also know a lot of writers who have health issues, and writing at home allows them to work when they feel good and then ease up a bit when they begin to feel lousy. You don't get that kind of flexibility when you work in an office.

There is a misconception that full-time bloggers are sitting in their PJs with the TV on all day. I'm not sure where this comes from because most of the bloggers I know are ambitious and never even watch TV during the day. They get dressed, schedule time for writing, and spend the rest of the day working on ways to grow their business. They're up, attentive, and driven.

A flexible schedule can actually mean longer hours, too. So on those days when you're fighting to meet a deadline or work ahead so you can take some time off later on, you'll feel as if your days are longer than when you were in the corporate world. But overall, the freedom to work more on some days and then take time off later on without getting permission can be a freeing feeling. You won't mind the longer days when you know you're the one in charge.

Building Your Blog Business

This book is aimed at making money from blogging, either for yourself for clients or a combination of the two. This means you should have a working knowledge of WordPress (which I highly recommend if you want to be a professional blogger) and that you perhaps even have a blog setup. But if you don't, I have a couple resources for you. I'll list them here and also in the "Blogging Resources" section at the end of this book.

I started my blogs using Blogger a decade ago and when it came to make the switch over to WordPress I studied various resources on the best way to do it. The good news is that I'm generally not a techie person and could do it easily, and if I can, then you will also have no problem. I used a series of videos found at the Become a Blogger site:

http://www.becomeablogger.com/resources/

and went through step by step until I had completed set up. I found this extremely easy to do because I could pause the video when I needed, rewind if I didn't catch something, and view anytime at my leisure.

Other resources I haven't used (but may be helpful to you) include:

- Michael Hyatt's guide to setting up a WordPress blog in just 20 minutes: http://michaelhyatt.com/ez-wordpress-setup.html

- Entrepreneur's Journey (a very helpful site for many reasons) offers tips on how to start a blog from scratch: http://www.entrepreneurs-journey.com/7698/how-to-start-a-blog-from-scratch/

- Mashable's how to set up a WordPress site: http://mashable.com/2013/06/11/wordpress-how-to/#

Blogging for Yourself or For a Client?

Every writer has a different formula on what makes blogging work for them. For some, blogging entirely for their own sites gives them income and satisfaction, and they leave it at that. Others get a thrill from being a part of a blogging team, getting a publishing credit, and having a presence on a recognized platform, so they enjoy blogging mostly for clients. Most writers, including me, fall somewhere between the two.

Benefits of Blogging for Yourself

Blogging really has become a revolution of sorts, giving everyone a voice they can share with the world. For freelancers, blogs offer a space for you to write the kind of posts you're most passionate about or those you want to show off as you apply for jobs.

I've started a variety of blogs over the years and have kept and maintained a handful of them. Many of my blogs are a decade old now and have proven to be very valuable to me for a variety of reasons. The benefits of having your own blog include:

- An online address that is yours, that readers know where to find you
- The freedom to post articles you're passionate about

- A way to build experience in order to apply for writing jobs (and an alternative to having "clips")
- All rules set by you (you can post as often as you like, have comments, close comments, and write in any style or voice you'd like)
- A place for readers to get to know you on your own terms
- A sense of community with other bloggers

You can also use your own blog to get work blogging for clients. Once upon a time you needed professional clips to get writing gigs, but today you can demonstrate the types of articles you'd like to write by putting them on your blog. Instead of copying a printed version of an article, you can attach URL's of blog posts in order to apply for jobs or pitch new clients.

Benefits of Blogging for Clients

Let's be clear, blogging today is simply writing online. Why do I make this distinction? Because some think blogging involves a less professional, more casual approach to writing or journalism. Blogging can take on whatever voice that is appropriate for the particular place you're writing for, but that doesn't mean the importance or accuracy is less professional. Don't confuse the more conversational tone and voice that bloggers sometimes use with a lack of knowledge.

When I started blogging, I was hired for all different kinds of jobs. I hadn't totally specialized in one field or another yet, so I had a range of assignments and the voice of each one was slightly different. On the health sites I wrote for I cited several sources and used third-person. For the entertainment blogs, the tone was very casual and chatty since I was writing for fans of celebrities. For the sports blogs, the voice was factual yet had an edge, a combination of stats and opinion. Each site had a different vibe and the voice of the blog needed to follow that. A blog on a news site is going to be different than one on an entertainment site, for instance.

As a professional blogger (or "problogger" as the term is often used) I need to vary the type of information shared and the way the information is conveyed, and this is much different than when I wrote for the print world. For instance, for some articles, my voice is a combination of first and third person. For relationship articles, I typically write in second person.

What's more, the need to change and personalize articles is much stronger online than in print. There are more people crowding the online space, and sometimes your voice will change just to distinguish your article as new and different. It used to be that everyone wrote in third person for major media outlets, but now the trend is a starting and ending paragraph or two in first person with the entire meat of the article in second or third.

Because of the sometimes casual (at least on the surface) voice, you might assume that blogging isn't as "serious" as offline article writing. But that's incorrect. Writers have adapted to the online world and the overall result is a more personal, close up approach to readers. This is a good thing, but should not diminish the importance of blogging. If you're going to blog to make money, you need to be aware that it's a business.

So being a freelance blogger simply means that you're a freelance writer whose articles show up online. Your writing will be different than if you had penned the article for the print word because people read and search for things differently online then they do with print.

Blogging for various clients and outlets has many advantages, including:

- A professional publishing credit
- Generally paid more money than if you'd blogged only for yourself
- Ability to interact with other writers on the site
- Building readership in a different way than if you had only blogged for yourself

- Working with professional editors

In the "Finding Work" section of this book I'll talk more about how to develop your client base. There are many ways to do it, some better than others. I'll give you places to search for work and ways to develop client relationships. For now, let's return to blogging for yourself.

What Does Your Blog Need to Have?

Not all blogs are created alike. But the successful blogs do share some of the same characteristics. If you see a blog you really like, take note of what draws your eye. Use the blogs you enjoy reading as inspiration for what to create for yourself. You can't (and shouldn't) copy someone else's form and content exactly, but you can look at what they have and use it to figure out what you can bring to your own site.

A Professional Look

Let's get the obvious things out of the way first. Your blog should look professional. Clients and readers do judge your site by how it looks. The good news is that today, setting up a site on WordPress with a professional template is inexpensive and easy to do, even for someone like me who is technologically challenged. I used **Studio Press** for most of my blogs and websites, but there are also plenty of free templates that can do the job as well. Check out **the WordPress site** for a **list of templates** you can load.

I highly recommend looking into the **Genesis Framework** from Studio Press as the basis for your site. With this child theme, you can easily customize your site for whatever functionality you need. Some of my sites are a combination blog and website, others are ecommerce heavy, and others have years and years' worth of blog posts combined with a shop. Each of my sites has its own look and feel and each were created using the Genesis Framework.

Once you have the Genesis Framework loaded, you can easily customize it and choose from a variety of themes available from Studio Press and a host of other designers. What's more, each of those themes is fully customizable, so what your site will look like is only limited by your own personality and ability.

Recently I spent several days updating themes on my sites, adding plugins, and learning some coding. This is totally out of my comfort zone, and yet, I did it. You can, too. There are things that are worth paying lots of money for a designer for, but there are also options if you aren't a designer and don't know how to build a site from scratch. You'll have to decide on what's worth your time and what you should outsource. I'll talk more about this in the "Maintaining Your Blog Business" section.

Helpful WordPress Plugins and Widgets

One reason I recommend WordPress so heavily is that it provides several plugin options you can download to change the look and functionality of your blog. For instance, do you want to have an ecommerce store? List Amazon products for sale as an affiliate? What about a newsletter signup spot? There are many plugins that can help.

I'm also a fan of how easy it is to change and move widgets on a WordPress site. This allows your site to be as unique as you care to make it, and if you're blogging for money, this is important. People want to visit a site that is unlike all the rest of the sites they see all the time. Here are some that I use:

Woo Commerce: This plugin and the related Genesis Connect for Woo Commerce, Regenerate Thumbnails, and Woo Commerce Menu Cart have been easy to use and update.

Easy Azon: For years, I added Amazon affiliate links manually, getting the pictures and then doing the physical link one slow, time-consuming stroke at a time. It slowed down my blogging and caused me to put off posts in some cases because I just didn't have the time.

For a long time, I had wanted to change the focus of my writing site to include information on various book lists, new releases every week, free Kindle books people could download that day, and I found it much too difficult to do manually. That's when I realized that I had to stop being so cheap and invest in my blogs. I purchased the Easy Azon plugin and found it easy to install and use. I especially like the image feature which allows me to pull a book cover right from Amazon without physically uploading it to my site. I use this feature every month when I do the **"Best Book Covers"** (http://workingwritersandbloggers.com/category/featur

ed-books/covers-i-love/) and **weekly new releases** (http://workingwritersandbloggers.com/category/books /) I list on my writing site.

Best of all, it allows for multi-site use, so I was able to use it when posting about my own books on my personal site.

Purchasing this plugin ended up saving me a lot of time, which as we know helps save us money. I have always been someone that is hesitant to spend money on things, even my business. I like to do things frugally, but there comes a time when spending a few dollars can save you in the long run.

Akismet: An essential plugin that helps with spam mail comments.

Contact Form: There are a variety of contact form plugins out there, and many of them work really great. If you're unsure, check to see which one is recommended to work with your individual theme. I use **Contact Form** 7 on all my blogs and have for years and it's worked out well.

Google Analytics by Yoast: Am I the only one that's had problems installing Google Analytics on my sites? Again, I'm a writer not a technie person. That's why

I appreciate this plugin, which does it easily for you and helps you track your site's performance.

Contextual Related Posts: It helps to have features and plugins that keep people there on your site. I used to use a related links plugin that showed people a graphic along with a link to a related post at the bottom of every new post. But lately I've used **this Contextual Related Posts** plugin and have found that it works quite well.

Image Widget: My entire world changed with this plugin. Well, just about! Before I loaded the **Image Widget plugin** to my site I would go through all different means of getting the HTML coding for pictures in order to do things like feature books or place ads on my site. Now, I just upload the picture and tell it where to link. Easy peasy. This is a favorite of mine.

Instagram Slider Widget: This is a new one for me, but since I've been hooked on Instagram I decided to install it on my personal and geek life sites. I like the variety and interest it adds to the front of my website and gives me one more place to update things without too much effort.

When I upload to Instagram, I will also usually post to at least one other source, like Facebook, Tumblr, or Twitter. I try not to duplicate social media posts because it can quickly turn readers off, so I vary where and how I'm posting things. With this plugin, my site gets an update every time I add something to Instagram, so even if you're not on Instagram you can get an idea of what's going on in my life. When blogging for a living, you have to think of ways to add technology and updates easily in order to keep your blog relevant.

WordPress Popular Posts: I like this plugin because you can set it to display the most popular posts for a variety of time frames and criteria, and also because the reader can easily see what others have found of interest recently on your site and click through.

Simple Social Icons: I like this plugin for adding all the links to my social media profiles easily and neatly onto the front page of my website. The icons show a graphic so the reader can click on your Facebook or Instagram profile, for instance, but it adds a clean look to your site. You don't need to write out a hyperlink that says "Follow me on Facebook" which can look unprofessional and clutter up your site. Best of all, the links and plugin are easy to use and install.

Author Avatars List: I use this on my Putting on the New site to show each writer's picture at the bottom of their posts. Great for a site with regular guest posts or just a variety of writers.

List Authors: This plugin helps you display posts by the writers on your site, either by post count, RSS, or name. It's another one I use for the Putting on the New site. When people click on the name of the author they are taken to a link that shows all the others posts. The author's short bio and photo is at the top, with all published posts below it. This is great for helping readers find their favorite writers work on a site with lots of different people, or for each writer to help promote their own posts rather than the entire site.

What Components Does Your Own Blog Need?

In order to make your blog attractive to readers and potential clients, it needs to have these components.

A "Hire Me" Page

Let clients know that you're available for hire. My hire me page:

http://cherieburbach.com/about/about-2/testimonials/

includes testimonials about my writing ability and work ethic, and tells people that I write for clients big and small.

I don't include a price list on my contact page, but I feel this is a personal preference. If you have work you do on a regular basis and want to give people an idea of what you'd charge, feel free to include it. I like to keep the parameters open because if there's a dream client that might pay less than I'd usually make but would otherwise be great exposure, I wouldn't want to have them see my rate schedule and get turned off by the fact that I'm outside their pay limit.

I've also worked with clients on a variety of options concerning pay, so that's another reason I don't want to list the actual figures. For instance, a few years ago someone hired me for a rate below my usual one. However, I took this job because I wanted to break into the subject area I was writing about and the contacts I made would help me going forward. For those reasons, this was a good job for me to have, but if I had listed my pay rate I probably wouldn't have gotten it. This is an entirely personal decision though. Sometimes posting your rates is very helpful because it shows people that while you work with a variety of clients, big and small, you don't work for peanuts. It can save you from saying no to people who have no idea what a professional writer costs today.

A Sample of Articles

Your blog should show a potential client what they would get if they hired you, so it makes sense to have some sample articles. These should be connected to your "hire me" page, either as samples you've done for other clients or those linked from your own site. Make it easy for a client to find your articles. Doing this step can save you from having to pitch them directly.

Sample articles that are done well can also attract clients to them with proper use of SEO. If a client is searching for a specific term and finds your site in their search, they'll look to you as an expert simply because you drew them to your article.

Articles that show what you're about can also attract readers and PR people. This is another way to make money. You can put ads on your site and make money as people click on the ads or visit the page. (I've got some sources to use for ads and affiliate income which I share in the "Finding Work" section of this book.) Or, if a PR person finds your site they may pitch you an opportunity of some sort. I've had this happen several times.

Once, a reporter Googled "dating expert" and my city and found me to do an on-camera interview. Another time, a producer found my site and asked me to consider hosting an upcoming TV show. I was asked to submit a video clip of myself and media package with my background. Both these opportunities arose because someone searched online and found me. It was as simple as that.

Other Places You've Worked

You don't have to (and shouldn't) list everything you've done, but you should give clients the impression that you can handle professional blogging. If you have paid or unpaid blogging experience for a client, list it somewhere on the blog, either on the "about you" page or on your "hire me" page. If you're an author (fiction or nonfiction) but haven't done freelance work yet, list the publishers you've contracted with. A publishing credit of any kind lets people know that you're a true professional.

Other Skills That Help With Blogging

Blogging and social media go hand in hand, so if you've got a lot of followers on Facebook or Twitter, list those on the "hire me" page along with a note that you'll promote the work you do for clients. If your website personally gets a lot of readers a month, you might want to share your stats somewhere on your blog as well. Showing people how many page views your site gets can help them decide if placing ad there would be appropriate. I do this on **my Working Writers site**, where I have various ad and social media packages people can purchase. Sharing my Twitter followers, page view numbers, and Facebook friends gives people an idea of the potential impact an ad on my site might have for their book or business.

Think of your "hire me" page as a way to show a client all you can possibly do for them, not just writing or blogging. The fact that you have limited knowledge in a certain area but possess excellent sample articles or high social media numbers may help get you a job you would have otherwise been overlooked for.

Don't forget to include the blogging platforms you've used. This little detail could give you the edge over another writer applying for the job. On my "hire me" page I have: "Cherie actively promotes the clients she works for as well as her own blogs. She has experience using Photoshop, WordPress, Moveable Type, Drupal, Skyword, and Typepad."

Define the Purpose of Your Blog

If you're reading all of this and still wondering how blogging might fit in with your career, don't worry. Blogs can change over time based on your own career and money making goals. You might start out wanting to write about one subject area but expand later on to other things. Or the opposite can occur, you start out with a blog where you want to write about lots of different subjects and find that you're mainly focused on one.

While the goal and purpose of your blog will change over time, you still need to define it so you can make the right choices. Don't be afraid to make mistakes or change direction, but do have a direction so you know where you want your blog (and blogging career) to go.

Maybe your blog will be a source to make money from all by itself. Or perhaps you'll be using it to attract new readers to your fiction work but also use it as a way to get freelance clients to notice you. Your blog can have multiple purposes.

If you've already started a blog and want to change focus, you can do that. Perhaps you started your blog years ago and now you want to make it more focused. When I started blogging, I really didn't know if I wanted to do it or not. I even started my blog with that very question in February of 2006:

"To blog or not to blog… that is the question.

> *I've belabored over this blog thing for quite a while now. Wondered if it's a good use of my time and would it take away from my other writing? But sometimes… a writer's just gotta WRITE… or get stuff off her chest… or whatnot.*
>
> *With that being said, my blog begins……..."*

I cringe when I read that now. What a stupid post. I could just delete it from my site, but why? It shows that I'm human, don't always know what to do, but I move forward the best way I can. My blog has continued to evolve and as it has I've streamlined things I wanted to do or realized I wanted to write a totally separate blog.

But what if you start a blog and it struggles to get off the ground, you might want to acknowledge that fact with readers. On my writing blog I talked about that dreaded "first post" and how much my blog has evolved since then. It's okay to change direction, but be sure your readers are along for the ride.

Even if you've got a few years of miscellaneous blog posts sitting there, it's not too late to do something entirely different from this point forward. For my personal blog I originally just made it about things going on in my writing or home life, but eventually I realized that sharing some of the posts and expertise I had about relationships or even writing was just as valuable. I changed it by adding those things to the blog as well, even though I had several years' worth of stuff that was different.

Once I changed my focus, however, I didn't look back. Starting awkwardly with your blog is one thing, but continually changing it is something else. Have a purpose in mind and stick with it. Often it takes several months (and even years) for readers to get used to the frequency and purpose of your new approach, so give them time to adjust before you decide you'd like to change it again. Think about what you most want readers and clients to know about you and your brand, and then blog with that purpose in mind.

Understand How Blogging Will Help You in Your Career

Even if the main purpose for buying this book was to learn how to attract freelance clients, you'll also reap additional benefits from your blog. Understand how blogging in general can help you in your career, because ultimately your site can be a source of referrals to the other things you do, thereby giving you more income on things like ebooks or articles. The indirect income you make from a blog can be just as valuable to you.

Too often someone (a publicist, agent, or editor) tells an author they "need to start a blog" and someone else tells them they can make money at it, and the author then muddles through the first few months or years' worth of posts trying to figure out what they want. They feel the pressure from their professional partners and instead of taking the time to think it all through, they forge ahead just to get the "blogging requirement" done.

A blog is valuable online real estate, so make sure you've got a clear picture in your mind of what you want it to be so you can then monetize it and attract readers.

Doing a Soft Blog Launch

I've started several new blogs because it's something I enjoy doing and truth be told, I like learning how to set up the sites. I don't always enjoy it while I'm in the process of learning, but later, when everything is set up, I take pride in knowing that I can change any feature on the site in an instant. I don't need to call a professional, pay them for their time, and then wait while they make the changes I want.

But one thing I've learned from starting up new blogs is that patience is your friend. If you've ever started a brand new blog, you know that those beginning days are really exciting. But before you go all out in getting the word out about your new blog, you'd be wise to do a soft launch. I've found this to be very helpful establishing the long-term success of your blog.

What's happens when people start up a new blog is you create a Facebook page, tweet out your first couple of posts, tell everyone to like your Facebook page, announce your new blog to your friends, and then they come and visit your blog and see one or two posts.

And that's it.

They'll probably never come back again.

The trouble is, you got everyone excited about your new blog but it was still in its infancy yet and wasn't a fully grown site. You need to allow it time to mature before you announce it.

By doing a soft launch, you write a bunch of posts and take time to slowly build a following naturally. No tweeting. No Facebook posts. Not yet.

When you've got enough posts to hold someone's attention, then you can promote like crazy.

Benefits of a Soft Blog Launch

A soft launch can:

- Help you develop a voice for your blog

- Secure any regular guest posters or co-writers

- Test out the placement and appropriateness of ads

- Build enough content to hold readers interest for more than just one page

- Test things like Networked Blogs or other automated services

- Determine if your blog has some search engine juice

A soft launch really just works out the kinks before you unwrap your blog to the public. Obviously, since a blog is public, some people will see your stuff, and that's okay. In fact, it's good. But you'll be saving the big marketing efforts for when your blog has matured.

How Long Should the Soft Launch Be?

Your soft launch should last just long enough for you to get your bearings. You should feel 100% positive that the blog you're starting is exactly what you want. Lengths vary depending on the blog and owner. Some of my blogs, especially Her Geek Life, took a year before I officially launched them. I kept changing things and adding different features to the blog and didn't want to officially announce it until I knew it was something I was happy with.

Other blogs were no-brainers, like my writing blog, Working Writers. I knew what I wanted to say and how I wanted to say it from day one. While that blog has changed focus slightly over the years to adapt to the changing demands of the writing and publishing world, I was confident launching it early on.

You'll know when it's time for the hard launch when you feel confident in your blog and your mindset goes from "I'm starting a blog on..." to "I *have* a blog on..." When you feel it's a steady blog, then go go go on the marketing front.

Ways to Make Your Blog Posts Stand Out

We're inundated with marketing today of all sorts. Everyone is shouting about books and blog posts on Twitter and Facebook, so it can be hard to get a potential reader's attention. One way to do that is through blog posts that stand out.

Special Graphics

Everyone uses the same boring graphics these days, don't they? There are several free places to get illustrations and pictures (and it's great to have these resources!) but a better option is to create your own graphics.

I like to use pictures from **Morguefile** or my own personal artwork and then use a pull quote from my article. Here's one example of that: http://puttingonthenew.com/2014/03/23/god-of-wonders-beyond-this-galaxy/

I created a separate graphic for a post where I asked bloggers for help in promoting my book (**seen here:** http://cherieburbach.com/2014/04/21/bloggers-i-need-your-help/), then used that same graphic as an ad on the side to keep it highlighted. It's colorful and draws your eye to the request.

I've illustrated some of my poetry like this:
http://cherieburbach.com/2014/04/10/like-old-men-in-rocking-chairs/ or used a completely new set of graphics to make it colorful and eye-catching, like this:

http://cherieburbach.com/2014/04/17/im-not-that-girl/. I like to use **Canva** or **Picmonkey** for things like this (both of these are free).

Visually Tell a Story With Pictures

Blogging doesn't always have to be word-focused. For posts where you can show a visual, use pictures to help tell your story. Part of my platform building strategy has been to show people a slice of my life, so I'll visually display the steps of a recipe I enjoyed making, like here:

http://cherieburbach.com/2014/01/08/black-bean-brownies/

or craft project I created, like here:

http://cherieburbach.com/2013/09/16/colorful-glass-mushrooms-for-the-garden/

Ann Voskamp (author of One Thousand Gifts) is great at visually telling a story on her blog, found here:

http://www.aholyexperience.com/

Although I'm not in love with the music that pops up automatically on her site, I do like the pictures she shares.

Know How to Format for the Web

People read differently on the Internet, so you need to change the way you write. Your writing needs to be clear, broken up into easily digestible pieces, and formatted for the screen. Specifically:

- Use bullet points to set off important points or lists
- Use bolded subheads to divide copy (and help with SEO)
- Break up long paragraphs

There's lots of argument about how long a post should be. Some places I write for require 700-1,000 words as a rule while others believe 300-500 words is optimal. My personal belief is that it takes a combination of long and short posts to keep a reader clicking through your site. The only thing that doesn't work? Thin, short content that doesn't hold a reader's attention (and gets you penalized from Google.)

Writing for the web isn't just SEO, it's formatting an article so someone's eyes can visually take it in. People often scan an article and don't read the entire thing on the web so your content needs to be something they can digest in pieces, scanning their eyes to over some things and reading others that interest them.

Use Getty Images

Getty (arguably the world's largest source for editorial photos) is now opening up thousands of photographs for use by bloggers. This is really exciting, because you now have access to the top celebrity, news, and stock photographs around... and... you have permission to use them. There are rules, of course, so be sure to follow them. (PC World has a great write up about how to use and attribute them here: http://www.pcworld.com/article/2105163/how-to-use-gettys-vast-collection-of-newly-free-pictures-on-your-website.html.)

The thing with Getty is that you need to abide by their rules. However, they make it very easy for you. Their photos are not embeddable (unless you pay for them) but you can use their html copy and place a very high-end cool editorial or creative photograph or graphic on your site. This is especially good news if you have a blog where you talk about celebrities, because editorial pictures like that are very expensive to use otherwise.

I also like the creative pictures, though, because I think they're higher quality than many I see on the other free sites. When every blogger seems to be pulling graphics and photos from the same places, this is an option that can allow you to stand apart. Your pictures alone can sometimes attract a reader's attention.

Use Pull Quotes

I mentioned pull quotes as part of a graphic, but they also work simply as a text box with words. This is especially helpful if you want to highlight a specific point or make sure someone that happens to be skimming (as people do on the Internet) at least catches the overall gist of what you're trying to say. This is a technique that magazine publishers do well. It draws your eye in and allows you to absorb key pieces of the article to remember for later.

This type of approach also helps with things like Pinterest. If a reader pins your article, they have a readymade graphic they can use (rather than having them choose a random graphic on your site instead.)

If you're the one promoting on Pinterest, a graphic like this can help others re-pin your article much more quickly than they would otherwise. People use Pinterest as a "save now, read later" type of holding place, and if you have a graphic that reminds them what the article is about, they'll be more apt to go back and read it later.

Writing With SEO In Mind

There's been a lot of misconceptions about SEO over the last couple of years. Some think that it's a trick to get more page views. Others think it's the magic key to perfect blog posts.

If you're going to blog, you need to know something about SEO, but you don't have to get spammy and aggressive about it. In fact, the best SEO strategy is one where you simply write well formatted and clear posts that readers will enjoy. Here's some tips I go back to again and again because they remain solid regardless of what the latest Google algorithm is.

Did you just wonder what a Google algorithm is? It's basically a computer program Google uses to help narrow down content for people.

Google changes their algorithms constantly, but two of the biggies over the last couple years were the Google Panda and Penguin rollouts. There are endless articles on these updates, which vary from the high level to deeply analytic, but for the average blogger what you need to know is that Google is committed to ranking higher quality articles and blog posts higher so that users can find them. Sounds pretty simple, right? But wait, it gets confusing. You might think your posts are well done but maybe they have too many ads, are formatted poorly, or just lacking in original information. If this is the case, Google may rank your post lower than someone else's, and users will have a harder time finding it.

As a professional blogger you will learn about various updates because they happen often and do affect your business. But they are always changing, so to list them here in detail would be futile. I can instead give you a list of resources to get some background and then places to follow to keep up on news that might be of use to your blog posts.

To read more:

- **Search Engine Land** is a great resource when you're a blogger, and their background and definition on the Panda update is solid: http://searchengineland.com/library/google/google-panda-update

- A comparison between Panda and Penguin from SEO Updates: http://seoupdates.info/difference-between-google-panda-and-google-penguin/

- The "winners and losers" of the Panda update: http://blog.searchmetrics.com/us/2014/09/26/panda-update-4-1-winners-losers-google-u-s/

If your eyes are glassing over, don't fret. I'll tell you what you need to know to make money as a blogger, and being able to predict SEO trends or Google data isn't part of it. Here's the method I have used for a long time as a blogger and one that has remained consistent in terms of search engine quality articles.

Write Your Article

First, write the article the way you want to write it. Too many bloggers focus on keywords and positioning of subtitles and not on the content of the article. The content is what people come for, and what will always remain relevant. Google updates may make your page views vary from time to time, but quality articles will always be the driving force. So write your article and then read it from the standpoint of an interested reader. This is when keywords come into play.

Finding Keywords

Keywords have become this slightly sinister concept with some people, but they are really just a way for people to find your work. They apply to sites, articles, and even books like this one. If you found this book as the result of a search, you probably used certain keywords to find it, like:

- how to make money blogging
- making money writing
- blogging income

or some combination of these. And guess what? These are the keywords! It's as simple as that. Now take this concept and apply it to a newly-written article. Did you use the right keywords so people can find your article?

A good resource for more on this is from Jeff Goins who talks about a **"non-robot" approach to keywords**: http://goinswriter.com/choosing-seo-keywords/ . I think the robot approach is what people most fear with keywords. Another good resource is from **Copyblogger**: http://www.copyblogger.com/seo-copywriting/.

In the method I promised you, when I finish writing that first draft, I look at the article from the perspective of a potential reader. Did I use jargon in the title or subheads that the average reader looking for this information would know? Did I try to inject humor into my title as therefore it doesn't make sense unless you know me personally or the subject I'm writing about in detail?

SEO needs to be straightforward, especially in the nonfiction world. This is important in the books you'll write or articles you'll post. For example, in my book on emotional affairs, I make it as obvious as possible what the book is about with my title: *Emotional Affairs: How to Prevent, Stop, and Move On From an Emotional Affair.*

Not an exciting title, but one that tells the reader exactly what they're going to get. This title is a good use of SEO. It's direct, simple, and doesn't confuse the readers. You should never write for keywords but rather include them to help your articles get discovered by the people who want to read your information the most.

Use Heads and Subheads

The experts go back and forth about how to use heads and subheads, but in my personal experience I've found them very valuable for SEO. Anything you bold or highlight gets attention from search engines. So as you break up your text with a subhead, make sure there is a keyword in it to make it worthwhile.

Subheads also help break up text nicely for those reading your article. We read differently online than we do with print, so subheads are a way for people to scan an article and read the parts they feel will answer their question. After all, most readers will probably come to your site through a search engine, and finding exactly what they're looking for is key to keeping them happy.

SEO for Blog Headings: Use Post Titles to Describe Yourself

I've found that descriptive titles and subtitles do help with SEO as well. Writers who would like to get established in a certain area should use their personal blog posts to describe something about themselves. For example, if the writer would like more jobs related to pillow stuffing, a blog post title could contain "Pillow Stuffing Expert Jane Doe Gives Tips" or "Jane Doe Talks to Class About Pillow Stuffing."

The more this combination is used, the more it is picked up on the Internet. Then, when someone searches for "pillow stuffing expert," Jane Doe would show up in search engines, along with her articles on the subject. Writers should use this example, changing out "pillow stuffing" for whatever area they are (or want to be established as) experts in.

SEO for Photos and Graphics

Readers are just as likely to find a particular article based on a photo as they are the articles themselves. Photos and graphics don't just add to a site's aesthetic beauty, they also provide additional elements for SEO. Bloggers should name their photos using keywords. For example, in the above example, a blogger could use the words "pillow stuffing" to name a photo rather than a general "photo123" or even "pillow."

Wordpress SEO Plugins

Bloggers on the WordPress platform can easily improve their SEO by installing one of many SEO plugins. Plugins are available at the WordPress site, or by searching for "SEO" on the plugins directory of any WordPress blog.

Plugins such as "Automatic SEO Links" and "Google XML Sitemaps" can assist bloggers with keywords, phrase linking, and anchor text. These plugins can help even veteran bloggers with their quest for search engine optimization.

It should also be noted that many WordPress templates are naturally optimized to appear well in a search also. Being mindful of SEO is important, but remember that the best way to optimize your site is to keep up on the latest techniques but always (always!) write for the reader first.

Writing for Multiple Blogs

If you're like most bloggers, once you start one blog you'll have the desire to start up another. They're freeing and fun and having an online space that's all your own can't be beat, no matter how you're using them. If you're just trying to make a few extra bucks, having more than one blog can give you a diverse side income. Diversity is good in the online world because things can change and you never want to be stuck with just one source of income.

I have several blogs and write for several clients out of need. The more I write, the more money I can make. But it does get daunting, especially if I'm unorganized or choose subjects that take me longer to research and write. As you build your client base and get more blogs to write for, you'll need some strategies for using your time efficiently. These are some methods I've found that work well.

Post Ahead

Blogging is much easier when your thoughts and energy are focused on one area. So rather than writing just one post a day, try to post ahead. By working on future posts you will ultimately write more material in a shorter amount of time. Not only that but you'll be able to take on new blogging jobs more easily.

Cluster Post

Cluster posting helps build on one idea to create several other ideas. You do this by starting with a topic and then looking for areas where you can expand on what you've written. For example, if you use a term in one post, use another post to dig deeper and define the term. If you use a particular example to reinforce your point, write another post giving more details on that example.

The best way to keep track of all this is to keep one file or notebook that you continually go back to before you create your posts. When you write one post, think about how you can quickly incorporate another idea before you move on to a different activity.

By far the biggest advantage in working this way is that you will be able to maximum your time. Instead of logging on to one blog, writing up a post and then logging off, you write several posts and then put them up when you have a block of them. This saves time logging on and off and also allows your creative side to pump out work. With this method, you don't need to stop and start again.

Cluster Posting and SEO

This technique also helps with SEO. By drilling down to the long-tail keywords you'll get more search engine juice for your posts than if you'd just covered a topic in broader terms. You'll have a better chance of reaching readers using their specific search engine terms than if you had limited yourself to just one post.

Keep an Online File of Ideas

Whenever you see a news article or website that would make a good topic to write about for your blog, copy the link to a Word or Excel file along with a quick note for a post idea. Then, when you have some time to write, open the file and allow your notes to spark your creative juices. Writing posts is so much easier when you have a bevy of ideas just waiting to be written out.

I keep documents like this for all my blogs, so when I'm ready to write for them I have several ideas to use as a jumping off point. Once I start writing, I allow cluster posting to expand on the original ideas I filed and soon I have a lot of content written as efficiently as possible.

Set Up Google Alerts

Set up an alert on Google for specific phrases that could help you get ideas for your blogs. For example, if you have a celebrity blog you could include the name of your celebrity, names of movies or albums, or even related people they know. If you write about books, you could set up an alert for specific authors or even a phrase, such as "new book reviews."

Google alerts will be delivered to your inbox. Each alert will notify you of any links, websites, or news items that have appeared in the last 24-hours with the specific topic or name you indicated. It's a good idea to set up a file on your computer where you can send each alert until you are ready to look through it.

Another good option to use is **Talkwalker Alerts**. It works just like Google Alerts and is also free.

Write Evergreen Posts

Posting ahead is easier if the type of material you write is evergreen. Evergreen posts stay topical and contain references and tips that are classic and not dependent on the news. You can take a newsy topic and approach it from an evergreen perspective or just fill up your blog with evergreen material that will keep readers coming back.

Create Theme Posts

Many bloggers create a theme for certain days of the week, such as "Wordless Wednesday" (in which a picture is posted without words), or "Thankful Thursday" (in which the blogger talks about things he or she is grateful for.) Posting ahead is easier if you have a regular theme you do because you'll be able to bookmark ideas for that theme and then pull them up when you need to write.

On my personal blog, I list "Things I Love" (http://cherieburbach.com/category/lifestyle/things-im-obsessed-with/) and also "Cool Things" (http://cherieburbach.com/category/lifestyle/cool-things-geek-life/) posts that are about various products I can't live without and stuff that if it happened would be really wonderful. Both these themes have been very well received.

Hashtags and Blogging

Using hashtags from Twitter, Facebook, or Instagram can help you come up with insightful blog posts as well. Check out **Instagram's Weekend Hashtag project** (http://blog.instagram.com/tagged/weekend-hashtag-project) or **Sprout Social's post** (http://sproutsocial.com/insights/twitter-hashtags/) on finding the best Twitter hashtag. Connecting your posts to a hashtag can be a good way to get some social media leverage and offer ideas for a set of themes to write about.

Create Top 10 Lists

Top ten lists of any type are not only a good way to get some headway on your blog, but are also generally considered evergreen and get picked up easily with search engine traffic. Readers enjoy them, especially when they are unique.

StumbleUpon

StumbleUpon is a really good resource for promoting your work, of course, but it's also great for getting ideas. Just take a "stumble" sometime and visit all the different sites out there, and you'll be inspired.

Comments and Emails

My readers give me a lot of ideas no matter where my articles appear. Some of them follow me to the articles I write for clients while others are loyal to one of my blogs. They are all passionate people who want to learn and get their points across, and I'm sure your own readers are the same. Use them!

Ask for Input

Well here's an obvious one. If you want ideas, ask for them. Find out what your readers are most curious about, or if they have questions you can answer.

Twitter

I use Twitter two different ways when it comes to ideas. I'll throw a question out there, like "What do #writers want to get more info on?" or I'll just do a search on a specific term and see what people are talking about. It's a wonderfully dynamic place to get and share ideas.

Take a Stand on Something in the News

If you see something in the news that can be related to your blog in some way, comment on it and make it a post. For example, when Netflix did their recent price hikes, I was able to relate that lesson to the freelance writing world.

Your Everyday Life

So much happens in your daily schedule you might miss some opportunities just because you're so busy. But pay attention, because little things can often kick off an idea for a post. I did that recently when we hired a plumber, and the way they went about charging me for service. (I'll share those thoughts later in the "Pricing Work" section of this book.)

Teach Something

Do you get people asking the same question over and over? Maybe it's time to tell what you've learned for everyone. That's what happened with one post I wrote about how to begin writing an ebook. I got that question over and over again from people, and while I don't have all the answers, I do have some information to get you on your way. I used that moment just to tell what I had learned myself on the subject, along with some tips I had picked up.

Don't assume everyone knows the same things you do. I learn all the time about writing and I do it every day! There are so many tips you can give someone, even when you don't think you're an "expert."

Share Your Experience

Another good way to teach is by sharing a recent learning experience of yours. If you just went through something where you needed to research and find out answers, share them! You'll save someone else time and you'll have some content for your site as well.

Finding Work

You don't need to have a blog before you apply for blogging work. It can help, especially if you want to showcase your knowledge on a specific subject, but it's not necessary. If you want to blog for clients, you need to be able to find the right jobs and contacts and pitch them.

While writing for clients has been the mainstay of my blogging income over the years, I also know that it's very beneficial to have your own blogs. Making money from a blog doesn't always have to be direct. You can profit from a great blog if it sells books or gets you great paying clients. This section will discuss ways to find work from clients, ideas for making money on your own blogs, and how to make an indirect profit from your blog.

First, client work.

Creating a Blogging Resume

A common question newbie freelancers have is: what kind of resume should I give a potential client? Unlike a traditional corporate letter, a writing resume is usually arranged to highlight subject area rather than years on a certain job. My resume is fine on its own, but I also customize it according to the client I'm pitching to or ad I'm applying for.

I've found that in applying for jobs it pays to give clients exactly what they're looking for with your resume. Don't make them hunt for the information they most require. Many freelance writing ads request a certain type of response, and writers need to follow this request to the letter in order to be considered.

Always read the ad closely before submitting your resume. Sometimes a client will put specific questions in their ad just to see if you're paying attention. If a client asks for four relevant writing links, highlight those right up front. If they want you to answer a specific question about what types of work you'd like to do for them, answer it and then offer up some article ideas. Be flexible with your resume so you can quickly give clients what they're looking for but not take up your whole day if you have several to send out. This is especially important if you're new and trying to apply for as many jobs as you can in order to get your blogging business off the ground quickly.

A solid yet flexible resume will help you pitch work, apply for jobs, contact clients, and even show potential advertisers for your blog what types of articles they can expect you to run on your site.

When I send my resume for a pitch or to apply for a gig, I start by expressing my interest and highlighting my experience, and then I get into specific sample articles and job history. I customize the links depending on what type of jobs I'm applying for or pitching. I also customize the beginning paragraph if I want to make sure a client has additional info about me that will help me get the job.

Somewhere in the middle, I highlight my experience. This would include jobs I've held, the types of work I did for each client, and how long I had that business relationship. Sometimes, I take out the books section if I feel that it wouldn't help me stand out to this particular client. Every business opportunity is different.

The samples I have are generally related to lifestyle and relationships since I specialize in those, but I have a much longer resume on my desk that includes a variety of links that showcase my business, sports, or health-related content.

I end the resume with some social media info so clients can see that I am active on these platforms.

Highlight Your Experience

Tailor your resume to answer the questions or concerns a client has indicated in their ad. Sometimes a potential client will only want to see the relevant experience a writer has for a certain writing style or subject matter. In these cases, your resume should include links to articles that showcase a specific knowledge area, focus, or theme. For example, employers may look for writers that can take news topics and create evergreen articles, write in the AP style, or have experience reporting on a certain topic.

For these types of jobs, answer the client's questions at the very beginning of the resume. Let's say a certain client asks for health care experience. A writer may start her resume like this:

Staff Writer for Health Today (June 2008-June 2014)

- Article Sample 1 (url link)
- Article Sample 2 (url link)

Other related writing would then follow:

- Health Blog Sample Article 1 (url link)
- News Blog Post on Health-Related Topic (url link)

Showcasing Social Networking Experience

I got into social media for work. I probably wouldn't be on any of the social media platforms if I hadn't been asked to do so years ago by various clients. I was reluctant at first, and over the years I've had to find ways to balance it out so that social media time doesn't overwhelm me.

Having said all that, though, I find that my presence on social media has helped me attract clients and promote my books and art. Many jobs, especially those for online writers, require a knowledge of social media. Clients want writers who can not only write great material but help promote it and they'll ask you for links to your Twitter, Facebook, and Pinterest handles so they can see that you're active in social networking.

In those cases, the client is looking for competent writing and awesome social networking skills. This means you should move your social media information to the top, and expand on it to fit the appropriate client. Always check to see what a client is already doing on social media so you can pitch them something that they'll instantly connect with. For instance, "I see you're using Twitter to promote your product, and I'd be happy to live tweet during XYZ TV Show to help you gain audience members." Or, "I'd be happy to share your Facebook page with my followers to help build your list."

If you have experience you think would help you stand out, be sure to share it. Such as, "I was able to grow my personal blog readership by tenfold in just two months by using Pinterest" or "My Twitter list has gained 10,000 organic followers in just three months. I can help build your list as well."

Never oversell your services or promise things you cannot for certain deliver, but do make your social media accomplishments known. You might want to break it out like:

- Twitter name: JaneDoe (10,000 followers)
- Facebook: JaneDoeWriter (1,000 fans)
- Jane Doe's Thoughts – personal blog (6,000 unique visitors per month)
- Jane's Craft Blog – personal blog (1,000 unique visitors and 10,000 hits per month)

Whether you start with social media info or job experience depends on the client and on your own background. If you don't have a lot of experience writing about a subject matter, highlight your accomplishments on growing a newsletter list or gaining social media followers first. Allow the client to see the best parts of your resume first and then, if they're interested, they can dig down to the other info about you.

Sending Pitch Letters of Introduction

I've found over the years that a pitch letter of introduction (where I combine ideas I have for possible blog posts while I introduce myself to an editor or hiring manager) is the most efficient way to contact new clients. I'm an introvert and cold calling a new client fills me with dread. I'm not good at it. What's more, I feel that the more I can put my experience and ideas out there first, the better the client will be at listening to me when I make a follow up call or email. So I like to send a pitch letter where I highlight the types of articles I'd like to write for them.

When I pitched the editor at NBC about a new site he was overseeing, I looked to see what types of articles and writers he had on there. I saw an opportunity to highlight my relationships experience, so when I sent my first pitch letter to him I listed five types of articles I'd like to write for him. Brainstorm a bit before you suggest something to an editor like this. If he or she likes it, you might be asked to write something right away. If not, learning to brainstorm can help you roll with the punches and quickly offer something new instead.

When I sent my pitch letter to NBC, there weren't any openings there for me, but the editor liked my ideas. I asked him if it would be okay if I followed up with the next month and he said that would be fine. So the next month, I went over the site again, and once again came up with five new article ideas I could write. I said:

"Last month you said you'd welcome a follow up from me about work. I appreciate that and thought of five potential articles I could write having to do with relationships. They are:"

And then with five bullet points I listed them. My editor still didn't have an opening for me, but a month or so later he did. I had asked him if I could follow up with him and my emails and ideas paid off. He hired me to write ten articles a month for him, and it was in my proposed subject area of relationships.

Finding the right person is the key to making this successful, but with LinkedIn and the Internet, it's never been easier to get the name and even email address of the person you need to contact. Never send a general letter as it will probably end up with the wrong person or even get thrown away.

A letter of introduction can make cold calling easier if you choose to follow up that way as it will help warm up the potential client for your pitch.

The key to a successful letter of introduction is not just highlighting your experience but listing the benefits to the client if they hire you. This is where you list your experience, ability to learn a blogging platform quickly, capability to promote posts through social media, or even get up to speed on the types of subjects your clients need.

A pitch letter of introduction is a short (no more than the equivalent of one-page correspondence) piece that highlights your publishing credits and background followed by blog post ideas you have for the client. Before you send this, scour the client's website. Note things like this:

- Do they update their blog on a regular basis? If not, mention that you could do a weekly blog for them.

- Are their blogs written well and sharable? Be careful if they already have someone writing them. You don't want to offend someone, so don't say, "I can do a better job writing your blog." Instead, this could be an opportunity of a different type, to work with their current blogger on developing share-worthy titles and stronger online content.

- Do they have a newsletter? You could offer to write posts that could be used for their newsletter, or you could do separate newsletter content for them.

- If they run a lifestyle or content site, is there a hole in coverage that you could fill? Pitch some ideas that would entice an editor to give you a shot.

You'd be surprised at how well a pitch letter can work. It's one of the ways to get blogging jobs that are high paying, $100 and more a blog post. That's because with a pitch letter you aren't competing against other writers or trying to fit your expertise into what the client is looking for. Instead, you're showing a client what you can offer and often it opens up ideas for them. They might not have thought about hiring someone until you came along.

Another reason pitch letters work so well is because the higher paying jobs are often not advertised. They can't be. If a company advertised a $100 per post job they'd have so many resumes they would be overwhelmed. Many times the companies that pay the best understand the value of good writers and know they won't necessarily find them by running an ad.

Pitch Letter Example

You have to address these letters to the right person in order for them to be effective. So that takes some digging. But you're a writer, and digging for facts is what you do. So this should be no problem.

How to do this? Look on their website or through LinkedIn first, but even if you find a name, call the company to make sure your contact info is current.

Then, in the first few lines, state why you are writing. For example, "I wanted to get in touch with you regarding blogging for your organization" or "I wanted to offer my freelance writing services to you in times of heavy workload or during the vacations of your staff."

The second paragraph should immediately talk about your experience. A writer should make this succinct and directly related to the work he or she is trying to obtain. For example, "I have worked for ABC Company and XYZ Firm, which also produce truck engines" or "I have worked with organizations similar in size and scope to your firm."

The next paragraph should list specific tasks that the writer has been successful with. These can be in paragraph form or bullet points. Typical points could be:

- Wrote press release for ABC Company to initiate PR campaign

- Helped XYZ Organization create a white paper outlining their new technical product
- Drafted direct mail copy for HGH Corporation

To wrap up the letter, highlight why hiring you would be a great idea. Perhaps you can get up and running quickly, thereby reducing training costs. Or maybe you can take over the workload during times when the company is understaffed. Each writer has a different benefit to provide for a company.

Make sure you list the pitch ideas you have in mind, and give some thought to this. Study the website so you get a feel for the type of articles the company uses now and might be receptive to.

For example:

"I have three ideas for future posts that I'd like to write for your firm. They are:

- How to Get a Small Business Loan
- 5 Behaviors That Successful Entrepreneurs Share
- 3 Top Causes of Burnout In a Small Business"

List three to five ideas they can think over. You don't have to have the articles written yet, but make sure whatever you pitch is something you can turn out in a short time if the client responds positively.

What If They Say No?

If the client doesn't respond, you could pitch at a later time with something else, but don't go beyond that. A lack of response usually means they just aren't interested.

However, if the client says no, see what else they tell you. One of my clients said "I wish I could hire you right now but I can't" which told me that if I stayed with him he'd find a way eventually to work it into his budget. For that client, I asked if I could just follow up with him every other month, and he agreed to this. If he'd have said no to the follow up, I'd have left it at that. (You definitely don't want to hound someone to the point that they get annoyed with you.)

If a client agrees to a follow up, it's because they're thinking about how they could fit you in to their current staff. This is a good thing, so don't give up.

Getting Clients to See the Benefits in Hiring a Telecommuter

Most writers love the flexibility of working from home, but there are still some clients that feel uncomfortable about it. Clients actually benefit from telecommuting in many ways, especially when they hire freelancers.

No Dedicated Office Space Needed

It makes no sense to have computer and office space set aside for freelancers who work at your office occasionally. When the freelance writer isn't there, it's a waste of money and the cubicle may sit empty.

No Traveling Costs

Many freelancers charge their clients for travel. I do, especially when their office is far away and driving there cuts into my productivity. Allowing freelancers to work from their home office eliminates that.

Clients Don't Need to Be Open in Order for Their Projects to Get Done

As a client, you might want a last-minute or weekend project completed. Are you going to open the office so the freelancer can work? How about just letting them get their work done at home while you close up shop on time?

No Interference From Your Own Staff

Depending on the project you have, hiring a freelancer can get tricky in terms of your own staff. Perhaps you're hiring for an overload of work, and some of your staff resent it. Or maybe you're hiring a freelancer because you don't think you have any qualified people to do the work. This can create tension in your office. With a telecommute arrangement you can keep the details to yourself.

Freelancers With the Right Expertise

You can hire a writer from anywhere when you work with them virtually. That means you can hire the very best freelancer for your niche or product area. Not all freelancers in your area are going to be qualified for what you need, but when you open up your hiring area to the entire country, you'll find someone with the perfect background and experience you need.

If you pitch a client for work (or even if they list a job ad somewhere) and they insist on having you come in all the time, mention the benefits of having you telecommute. It could help you convince them that it's in both of your best interests for you to work from your home office.

Where Do You Start to Look for Work?

The biggest question newbie writers ask me is where do you start? It's overwhelming to look for work, especially when you are new and unsure how to pitch, unsure of your own rates, etc. That was one of the problems I had when I first started out. I had no problem getting meetings with people but was not confident enough with the rates I had set for myself. So without the client even questioning my rates, I would lower them before the meeting was even over! Obviously, I don't do this anymore. I would have never stayed in business for a decade if I had kept that up.

Job ads can seem like a much easier way to get gigs when you're a newbie, but conventional wisdom has been that applying for work this way is the worst way to do it. I don't agree with this. It's not the best way but it isn't the worst way, either. Plus, when you're a newbie, you can actually learn a lot about the market by studying job ads and even applying for work.

The 10 Best Job Boards to Find Freelance Work

My favorite way to get freelance jobs is by networking and contacting editors directly. But when I was a newbie, I skimmed the job ads. In fact, I still skim them now so I can get an idea of what's out there. Every once in a while I apply for one or two of them, and every once in a while I get a good gig that way. I've learned to make job ads work for me, and I'll tell you things to look for and how to apply to give yourself the best possible chance to get them.

The perception is that job ads only want to attract writers who are new and will presumably work for a low rate. But I've found that sometimes a great paying client really doesn't know how to find a writer so they end up posting something on a place like Craigslist or some other ad site! I found one of my best paying gigs by applying for a job that way.

It isn't always the newbies who apply for work this way. Sometimes an experienced writer who has had a bunch of long-term clients might find themselves needing more work and feeling out of touch with the market. They'll go to the job ads to see what's out there. Where would they look? Where should you?

There are tons of great places, but here are ten of my favorite sites to look for work.

- Freelance Job Openings:
  http://www.freelancejobopenings.com/

- Online Writing Jobs: http://www.freelancewriting.com/freelancejobs/onlinewritingjobs.php
- Problogger: http://jobs.problogger.net/
- Blogger Jobs: http://www.bloggerjobs.biz/category/blogger-jobs/
- Whisper Jobs: http://ed2010.com/whisper-jobs/
- Dice: http://www.dice.com/
- Journalism Jobs: http://www.journalismjobs.com/index.php
- Media Bistro: http://www.mediabistro.com/joblistings/
- All Indie Writers: http://allindiewriters.com/freelance-writing-jobs/
- Indeed: http://www.indeed.com/

Things Every Job Ad Should Include (But Usually Don't)

Not all job ads are created equal. That's because people have different levels of writing skills and don't always know which types of things to put in an ad. Or, it's because they're trying to scam writers and therefore are not straightforward with their information. This is another reason why ads are a dangerous place. Here are some things that are typically left off job ads, which make it harder to apply and can be a time suck for you if you try to find out more.

Rates and Scope of Work

I wish I could say that only the spammy people failed to list rates, but the reality is that different types of clients leave off rates for a variety of reasons. I would encourage any client to make their rates known, but then again I leave off rates on my own "hire me" page, so perhaps there is a good reason for it.

Still, as a writer it's frustrating to pull all your material together and format it exactly as the client wants only to find out the client is paying peanuts.

Also, clients sometimes fall flat when listing the entire scope of work required for a job. Maybe they themselves really aren't sure. I've applied for many jobs that said one thing when I applied, but when I was called for an interview had several more requirements tacked on.

Clients shouldn't just say they are hiring a "blogger" without describing everything they expect that blogger to do. For instance, will they need to find pictures on their own, do interviews, extensive research…? This should be included in the ad, but the reality is that as a writer you'll have to ask them about it.

The Exact Requirements Needed

I also find language that dares the writer to apply annoying. It's one thing to state your needs and another to make it sound like a challenge. I'll usually skip ads that say:

- "Wow us with your samples"
- "Show us something we've never seen before"
- "Requirements? Pitch something we've never thought of"

My advice? Skip these ads as well, and if they list a company name make note of it. Companies like this tend to go through writers quickly so you don't want to get caught in the shuffle. If you see future ads from them you'll know not to even bother applying.

A Clear Vision of Who the Clients Is

Another weird thing I've seen lately are clients who don't want to say who they are because they're afraid they'll be inundated with ads. So instead they say things like, "Trust us, we're big" or "You'd know our site if we listed it."

Well list it then.

My opinion is that if you're looking for writers, we don't know your site. Most sites that don't need to advertise for writers are well known and get pitched to often. They generally don't place ads (which is why pitching is still the best way to get work.)

Professional Tone

Another pet peeve of mine is when an ad has some snotty language in it, like:

- "Don't apply if you can't follow rules"
- "If you don't follow these requirements to the letter your application will be deleted without a second thought"
- "If we have to hold your hand, apply elsewhere"

Who wants to apply for that? Even I'm qualified for the jobs listed, I'll skip an ad like this. It just gives me a bad impression about the client overall. These types of clients show me right off the bat that they will be as arrogant and uncooperative as possible.

But then again, seeing a client's bad attitude in an ad can save you aggravation down the road. The beginning of any relationship should be a positive one, before there are misunderstandings or disagreements. So if a job ad sounds like the person you'd be working with is a real pain, pay attention to that. This is one way job ads can give you a clue about the client you'd be working with.

Here's some more ways to use job ads.

- To watch for trends in hiring freelancers
- Other "related" jobs (like editors and designers) so I have an idea of where I could pitch work (If a company is hiring editors, it's only a matter of time before they start looking for writers)
- New websites (because sometimes those hiring writers don't know how else to attract writers, and they post ads instead.)

My advice? You should still skim the job ads if you want, but don't use it as your main source of finding work.

Be Cautious If You See These Things In a Job Ad

I've given you some of my pet peeves with job ads, but there are some things you should watch for because they could mean a bad experience for you. Here are some phrases to watch out for.

You Can Make Up To...

If someone is giving you a figure you can possibly make per day, more than likely they are looking for volume writing. Volume over quality. Usually these types of jobs require some ridiculous amount of articles per day, and if you meet this ridiculous number you can make X. Except that if you actually divide your time into X, your pay is peanuts.

Don't work for peanuts.

Good for Stay at Home Moms or College Students

These words are code for "we don't pay very much, but it might be something for people with nothing better to do." The ironic part of course is that stay at home moms and college students have a lot better to do than waste their time on jobs that don't pay! Clients that value skilled writers are not putting this stipulation in their job ads.

Only Experienced Writers Need Apply

A genuine outfit that pay writers well doesn't have to put this in their job ad. They post their ads and skilled writers apply. They search through the applications so that they can hire the most skilled in their opinion. That's it.

There are some jobs that are going to attract newer writers, because the job ads are written too vaguely, or the person hiring wants the moon and won't pay for it. These are the types of clients that put this verbiage into their ad.

Compensation: You Tell Me

I've actually seen quite a few ads that ask writers to tell them what a project is worth. Its fine to give a client your rate, but it is irresponsible for them to ask this from a job ad. In order to accurately quote a rate, you need to know all the specifics, and job ads rarely provide them. You need to know things like:

- The tone and approach of the writing required (press release versus conversational blog post versus sales copy versus web writing)
- How much research time you need to do
- Whether you need photos or specific sources
- The end-goal of the writing project
- Feedback or approval time
- Social networking requirements

- and on and on.

You can give a client a range when asked this in an ad, but chances are they are looking for the cheapest rate. If an ad is promising, what I do instead is tell them I'd be happy to give them my rate after I talk to them about the true scope of the job.

Ads That Are Placed On Every Job Board Imaginable

Sometimes a client just wants writers. Period. Any old writers. Can you type? We'll hire you. If they are advertising on every job board you see, it's a signal that they may be looking for quantity of writers. (Which usually translates to low pay.) Use caution if you see this.

Job Ads That Continually Pop Up

This means that they are either expanding (which is good), or they can't keep writers on their staff (which is not good.) My advice with these types of ads is to apply if you feel like it could lead to something, but feel free to ask them at some point what happened to the other writer. I usually say, "I noticed this job ad was up a few months ago. Can you tell me why it is open again so soon? I'd like to establish a long-term relationship with you."

Listen to what they say. Good things you want to hear are:

- We promoted that writer
- They are writing for another segment of ours
- We are growing and need more talent.

Things you don't want to hear include:

- Our former writer had no work ethic
- That person just didn't work out
- That person went on to greener pastures.

These are all code for some type of problem. Was the problem the writer or the client? You need to dig deeper.

Job Ads That Continually Run

Perhaps a client only advertises on one or two job boards, but they advertise constantly for the same job. What does that mean? It may again mean they are only concerned with growth (more writers more writers more writers!) or that they go through writers so fast they never bother taking the ad down.

When I worked heavily in the print world, I saw an ad for writers that ran continually in one magazine. I applied and after a few months I got hired to write a few pieces. Then, I got a call that "a writer of theirs flaked" and they needed a piece turned in by the next day in order to meet their print deadline! I immediately wondered what happened because saying a writer "flakes" could mean a number of things. But I needed the work, so I took the assignment.

These people paid a month after publication (which was already a month out.) That means if I wrote a piece in January, it would run in February and I'd get paid in March. So when my payments should have started coming in, I noticed my little old mailbox was quiet. When I called to find out, I was told I hadn't submitted my invoice to them. (I had.) I submitted another one, and was told they were having "cash flow problems" and that my payments would arrive "when they could get them." I waited. My payments still didn't come.

When I called again, they stressed that they were a "small outfit" and only had one person that could cut checks and that person didn't come in very often!

See the problem? They advertised to new writers continually so they could use their two-month "float" time to get a few more articles from someone new before they had to start paying. I wonder how many writers were not as persistent as I was in getting their payment. Perhaps the writer who "flaked" really just got tired of doing work and not getting paid for it.

In the end, I told them that I would happily come and sit in their office until they could find the time to cut the series of checks I was owed. (This advice was from my husband, who was fully prepared to sit there for me! Dontcha love that? I would have never been so bold. However, it worked. I got my checks finally after that, but made sure I turned down any future assignments.)

Bottom line, navigating the job board waters is not easy, but you can get the occasional gig that does pay. Do some sleuthing to find them.

A Better Way to Find Freelance Blogging Jobs

Now that we've talked about ads, let's get into other, better ways to find work. I've found that the best thing you can do when pitching and searching for work is just be consistent. Do it little by little, even when you're busy.

If you consistently do certain things you will find work. It's that simple. If you do it here and there, you'll find work here and there. If you do it when you need work, you'll have a harder time finding great jobs because you'll grab for things that are lower paying just to pay bills. (And we've all been there.)

Here's what I do on a regular basis:

Watch for News of Website Launches

Sometimes jobs aren't advertised, but you can find out about them just by paying attention. Subscribe to places like Mashable and Media Bistro, and you'll be alerted when new sites are launched. New sites generally need writers, so approach them. Find out if they are hiring and offer a sample of what you could do for them.

Contact Websites

If you see a website that you think you could add some expertise to, contact them. They can only say no, but you'd be surprised at how many times they might say yes. Carefully word your letter. Don't say "Your website sucks and I could do so much better" but rather list your qualifications and give them an idea of what you could bring. Write up and sample post or two.

Search "Write for Us" Pages

You'd be surprised what surfaces when you do this. Again, look through the site before you apply. Sometimes people will say "write for us" and they mean unpaid work. Obviously, if you're looking for paid work, unpaid doesn't work.

Subscribe to Writers Market

I used **Writers Market** (http://www.writersmarket.com/) for years, especially in my earlier days of freelancing. I found the $6 monthly fee for the online database a real bargain. One word of caution, though. While the site does a great job of listing contact people, it's not always updated. (People move jobs quickly in the publishing world.) When you find a place you'd like to pitch, look them up on Linked In or call the magazine instead. Directing your inquiry to the right person is very important.

Get to Know Other Bloggers

Bloggers love to recommend each other and share the wealth. They are wonderful at telling others about jobs, even when they are kind of interested in applying themselves. That's because blogging is one of those rare worlds where the more you support your fellow writer, the better it is for you in the long run.

If you don't know of any other bloggers right now, start looking for a few online. Many bloggers love sharing what they make or the best places to get high paying gigs. For instance, **writer Luke O'Neil shared his income** (http://bullettmedia.com/article/much-freelance-writer-makes/) and places he worked at, Carol Tice has a list of 140 places that pay writers (http://www.makealivingwriting.com/140-websites-that-pay-writers-updated-2014/), and the awesome Who Pays Writers site (http://whopays.scratchmag.net/) talks about real pay listed anonymously by real writers.

Watch the News for Opportunities

Sometimes an existing publication, one that never hired a freelancer ever will suddenly get into a new business line and need a writer. The thing is, the business will be launched first, and then they'll start thinking about hiring the writer. Look for opportunities like this in the news so you can be the first one to send something in rather than waiting until they list something.

Watch for Editors That Change Jobs

When a new editor takes over for a magazine or website, they sometimes want to freshen things up. This is the perfect time to send your stuff in! I find out about job changes like this on sites like Media Bistro, general news sites, and even sometimes LinkedIn.

When You're at a Company Doing Business

Occasionally, we'll go to a place of business and I'll ask if they hire freelancers. These are usually smaller companies in our area but you'd be surprised at how positively people respond. At the very least they give me the right person to follow up with (saving me a phone call to find out) or they take my business card.

Follow Up With Former Employers

When I first started freelancing, I went to all my old employers and told them I was now freelancing. You have to make sure you're in good standing with your former companies in order for this to work! A former employer of mine was actually my first freelance writing client. I told them I was now freelancing and they immediately had a few projects they wanted to hand over.

Companies often have one or two projects that get pushed to the side because they don't have the staff or time to get to them, and one reason they get neglected is because the company just doesn't have a freelance name on file to call for help. You can fill that slot.

Applying for Jobs Without Clips

Recently I gave a talk for a group of aspiring writers, and I got several questions about "clips." Clips are past writing assignments, either in print or online, that are similar to the job advertised. The term "clip" comes from the old days when everything was in print, and you had to clip out the article and keep it in a folder or copy it and give it to a potential client. Clips are one way to showcase previous work experience so your client can decide if you'll be the right person for their particular project.

But what if you don't have any clips? In other words, what if you're a brand new writer, or you've never written in the area that you are applying? Here are some ways new and unpublished writers can still show a potential client he has the experience necessary to do the job.

Write a Sample Article

When an employer asks for clips, it's because they want to see if a freelancer can write in a particular style or subject matter. So if a new writer doesn't have an existing article to showcase, he should create one from scratch. Doing a bit of research on the client and what type of writing they generally publish will help in this area.

Writers should polish the sample piece with the intent that it may help them land the job. They should also be honest with a client and let them know that the clip is a sample (and thus unpublished) but stress that they understand the quality of writing needed to do the job. Most employers will appreciate a new writer making this extra effort.

Be cautious with sample articles! Don't write up articles that an employer can use for free. Some places ask for samples on a regular basis for writers and then try and use them. Make sure your sample is yours and that the client doesn't keep it for their own purposes.

Write Blog Articles That Show Level of Expertise

Another option is to let your blog speak for you. Writers today have an advantage over those who started years ago in that they can publish their work online, publicize it, and gain readers even before they get paid as a freelancer.

To make your blog work for you, make sure it really shows off the type of work and expertise you specialize in (or want to specialize in). This will come in handy when you see a job you'd like to apply for. If there is a particular blog post you think will showcase your work, include it as part of your writing resume. This will give a client a sense that you understand the area that you are applying for.

Another way to get your blog to work for you is to showcase your readership. If you can show a client that you have the traffic numbers and reader comments for your own blogs, the perception is that you'll be able to do that for their site as well.

Writing Work for Nonprofits and Volunteer Organizations

Just because a writer has yet to be paid doesn't mean he lacks the right experience. Any previous volunteer or unpaid writing can be used as sample clips. Offering writing services for free is a great way to build rapport and a future relationship that can turn into a paying client one day.

Freelance Writing Guest Posts

Writing guest posts are a good way to get back links for a blog or website, gain experience, and showcase writing skills. Doing a guest post may even help land a job for a similar website or organization. The great thing about writing opportunities is that you never know where they can come from.

Each assignment and article builds on the next, and it all starts with a few articles.

Be a Writer That Editors Want to Work With

People ask me constantly where they can find writing jobs, but here's something we don't talk about enough: If you're a writer that is easy to work with, work will find you. People will seek you out. Here are a few ways you can be a writer that every editor wants to work with.

Get Your Work Done Early

Forget "on time." Take the deadline you have and move it up. There's your real deadline. Get it done early so your editor doesn't have to hound you or waste time finding out where you are with the work.

Be Flexible

Things change. The writing world is nothing but change these days. So go with it. Don't get comfortable. If you have a job you like right now, be glad. But be prepared for things to change.

Don't Complain

Professional writers work and don't complain. They might not like everything that's handed them (in fact, there's a good chance they won't like it) but they won't complain about it to the editor (or on Facebook, Twitter, or to a group of other writers). If you've gotta vent, do it with a trusted friend.

Embrace the Fact That Your Work Needs to Be Edited

Everyone gets edited, but some writers really take offense at this. They shouldn't. It's part of the process. Even if you never complain to your editor, the fact that you don't like editing or are resisting it in some way will come across to them. Learn to accept and embrace editing and you'll have an easier time working with someone.

Talk Through Things

If you work with one editor long enough you'll probably develop a rapport where you can talk through things. Even then, pick your battles. There are genuinely some times when things should not be changed. Perhaps your editor doesn't have the 411 on the background, and you can explain why things should stay just as they are.

But be cautious about this and don't dig your heels in on everything. Pray on the advice you're being given and think about it a while before you decide to push back.

How to Get a Steady Stream of Writing Clients

Getting new clients is the key to building your freelance writing business. It isn't easy to find people that pay and treat you well, but trust me, they are out there. Having quality clients you enjoy working with is half the battle of building your business. Here are some tips I've found helpful as I've built my own freelance writing biz.

Send Out Letters of Introduction Every Week

In the beginning, I sent out three new letters of introduction every single week. Three might not sound like a lot, but I researched them to find out the best person to send to and what they might need in terms of writing assistance. I wanted to make the letters as targeted as possible.

I sent out letters of introduction for a couple reasons. The first was that it acted as an introduction for when I placed calls. (I hate cold calling.) Second was that I usually got a response of some type. I didn't always get a "we'll hire you!" response, but I did get a "thanks, we have an in-house staff" or whatever type of response. The point is, I made contact and someone noticed. Making contact is half the battle, because if they can't use your services now, there still might be an opportunity down the road.

Join a Business Group

I've joined many business groups over the years and have found them a great place to find clients on a regular basis. As part of the group you'll be talking about yourself and the work you do anyways, and in the process someone in that group may need a writer or know someone who does.

Ask for Referrals from Existing Clients

You know all those clients you work with now that love you to pieces? Ask them for a referral! Getting new clients is something that usually starts slow, and builds over time. As time goes on, it gets easier to find people to hire you because you have connections in place. Once you have a steady stream of clients, you will have an easier time picking and choosing the kind of projects you'd like to work on.

Establish Relationships and Banish the Feast or Famine Attitude of Writing

There's a perception that freelancing is feast or famine, meaning sometimes you'll be inundated with assignments and other times you'll be scrounging for work. I'm here to tell you, it doesn't have to be this way. You can combat that somewhat by being consistent about getting clients and having work in the pipeline, but even with that clients can change their budgets, the market can change, and things can happen that prevent you from getting the work you want.

I've tried to avoid the ups and downs by establishing relationships with clients, meaning that instead of one-off assignments I pitch them ongoing work right from the beginning. This is especially important for things like blogs or publicity because it takes time to build effectiveness over time. If a company is just looking for "some blog traffic" and hires me occasionally to write something here and there, they won't see the same benefits as they would if they hired me to write regular blog posts at least once or twice a week followed by promotion on social media.

Or, if a company is looking for publicity, they'd be better off hiring me to write regular press releases and pitch editors for articles about their accomplishments rather than one press release each time they feel they have something newsy to announce.

This approach benefits me as well. If I can stress the importance of a consistent relationship with them I can get regular work and avoid some of the fickleness of the freelance life. So when I approach a client, I always do it with the relationship in mind. I will quote my rates based on a minimum two or three month contract for a series of regular blog posts, or a year-long agreement to write a certain number of press releases, or an ongoing agreement for a set number of posts each month.

With this type of arrangement, I am guaranteed a certain amount of money for as long as the agreement is in effect. I then continue to add clients until I have a certain amount of combined "salary" with all my gigs. While things can change, this approach helps me budget my money and also keep control of my schedule. When I know which types of assignments I have coming up, I can better work ahead for things like days off and I know how much my schedule can handle if I try and add new clients to the mix.

Making Money From Your Own Blogs

Can you make a living just from your own blogs? Yes. Or, you can make a side income. Or, you can combine your blog income with that of your books or freelancing writing income. Variety is really key when you're a writer, so the more you can diversify (either by subject matter, clients, or ways to make money) the better you'll be able to roll with changes in the market.

Here are some ways to make money from (or monetize) your blogs.

Affiliate Income

This is one of the most popular ways to make money from a blog mainly because it's easy to do. Before you attempt to earn money this way, do some investigating on which types of revenue might work best for your particular site. You can't just slap some affiliate ads on there that don't relate and expect them to do well. Ads of any type need to be matched to the needs of your readers.

I used to shy away from most types of affiliate income because I was afraid of "pushing" stuff on my readers. Then I realized I naturally talked about certain products and services, and began to tailor my approach to finding just the right type of affiliate and only placing ads for those particular things. This made a huge difference in my success at earning affiliate income.

Also, sometimes affiliates do take some time to build. So you can try out different methods but give it a little time and go slowly. I have five different types of sites and can tell you that each one responds to affiliates a little differently. An affiliate that really does well on one site won't work at all on another. Finding the right products or systems may take some time before you find the right balance for your particular blog.

Here are some popular affiliates that bloggers use. Please note, I don't use all these and can't recommend which ones would work well for you. I can only point you in the direction where you can find out more. Every blog is different. For most of these sites you'll need to sign up for an account and then choose a way to be paid, usually through PayPal or direct deposit.

Google Adsense – This is one of the most popular affiliate programs in part because it's so easy to use. Simply place the right html code (and there are a variety of blocks to choose from) and each day you'll see your results. I like them because they pay on time and without hassle. Their ads usually match my audience well.

CJ Affiliate by Conversant (Formerly Commission Junction) – I know bloggers that use this site and do very well with it. I used them for quite a long time but found that it wasn't the right fit for my types of blogs.

ClickBank – With ClickBank, you sign up for an account and then chose different services to promote on your blog. When someone buys one, you get a certain part of the sale. I like the variety of subject areas on this site, although from my experience most of the products are ebooks. Still, depending on the subject matter of your blog, you may find one or two hot sellers that really resonate with your readers.

Share A Sale – A lot of popular brands and products on this site which do seem to differ from the other affiliate sites I've seen.

Amazon Affiliates – Also a top favorite, and one that, while it seems to take time to build, does add up over time. They pay a variety of ways, even direct deposit to your account. The great part about Amazon is that they really do have just about everything available on their site, so no matter what your blog is about you'll probably find something to promote there. I find that I naturally talk about books I like or movies I've enjoyed so these seem to fit well with this affiliate.

Your Favorite Book or Product's Private Affiliate Program

Not all affiliates are going to be listed with a network and therefore will have their own private affiliate signup. Check out a few of your favorite writers or brands and see which might have a program where they pay you for promoting their products. It will often be listed on their website with a link that says "We'll pay you to promote us" or "Join our affiliate program."

While an affiliate network like ClickBank or Share A Sale will combine payments for all the different products you promote (which is one advantage to using this type of system) a standalone affiliate program can also work well if you really love and promote a certain type of product and talk about it a lot.

Ways to Make Money Using Affiliates

When you're building up your blog, it can be frustrating when you keep hearing about bloggers making a lot of money with certain affiliates while you're struggling to get off the ground. You can help your chances of success by:

Always Thinking of Your Readers First

The number one rule I keep going back to with affiliate income is that it has to be adding value for my readers. I don't just cram miscellaneous ads all over that have nothing to do with my site or their interests.

Write Blog Posts That Review or Give Tutorials About the Affiliate's Product

It makes sense that if you're going to promote something, you might as well talk about it. Again, make sure a review is appropriate for your audience. For example, you may want to write a book review for a certain book you've read that you're also an affiliate for. Be honest in your review, of course, but give information that can help answers questions about whether or not the book is right for your particular reader.

If there is a product that is fairly complicated or one that you're getting a lot of questions on, create a detailed step by step with a link to buy at the end. This may give someone confidence to try the product if they know how to set it up and use it. This type of thing works well for things like WordPress plugins, for example, where bloggers talk about their experience in setting up the product so others who purchase it (perhaps with the affiliate link) will have an easier time using the product.

Posts with reviews or tutorials are also great for SEO. They are valuable blog content regardless if someone using the affiliate link to buy something because they draw readers to your site and keep your blog's authority high.

Position the Affiliates Correctly

Adsense, for example, has recommendations for how to position ads so they will work better for your site. Use these recommendations because they can be very helpful. I was able to greatly increase my payout a while back because I changed the positioning of my ad blocks.

Use a Graphic or Create an Ad

Most affiliates will offer graphics of some type to help you promote their product. Using different affiliates can help you promote products in a different way. While an inline text link may be useful for some readers, a graphic might be more inviting for others.

Use the Tips and Tutorials for the Products When Promoting

Some products give you things like promotional ideas or tips on how to promote, and while I'm not a fan of these myself I do know bloggers who have really ramped up their income by taking special ecourses and watching video tutorials on how to promote specific products.

Give It Time

One of the most frustrating things about being an affiliate is putting all the ads and shout outs on your blog and then waiting… and seeing no return. While you can't wait forever, I have noticed that it does take several months for some affiliates to start earning for you. So before you decide to pull the plug and change out the info to a new affiliate, analyze any data or trends you see to determine if you should wait a bit longer.

I've noticed that some affiliates take a while because your readers are getting used to them. They may click a few times on things and not buy, and then in time you'll see a sudden burst of activity where sales are being made. Perhaps the reader is leery of the affiliates and looking for more info, so they wait. Perhaps a new reader doesn't know you or your reputation yet so they wait until they read your blog for a while before clicking some of the links. Waiting may be a good option but you won't know unless you test things out.

What Happens If Readers Leave When You Add Affiliates?

When you try anything new out on your blog, you may irritate a few of your readers. So adding affiliate income sources might anger some of them and they'll leave. What I've found, however, is that most readers understand that you're trying to make money, you're trying to be helpful (and only recommending things you think they'll like) and you're trying to stay current.

I haven't noticed readers unsubscribing or having my stats go down just because I've added affiliates. I add them slowly in order to determine their effectiveness and so readers won't be inundated with tons of changes on my site at once. Ultimately I want my sites to be helpful to readers, and I look for material and affiliates that fill that requirement.

If you notice a lot of readers leaving your site after you add affiliates, you have some options.

Keep Things the Same

You can make a choice that if you want to start earning money on your blogs you will be using affiliates of some sort. That means that you'll want readers who get that you're trying to balance the desire to earn income (and therefore keep writing for your blog) while being helpful and interesting. So you can always decide that regardless if readers leave, you'll keep trying out different ways to make money. Once you settle in on the right affiliate choices for your blog, your readers may come back. You never know.

Address the Issue

I don't recommend this, but I have seen bloggers address the changes on their blog, asking for readers time and patience as they try out new programs. The reason I think it's a bad idea is because it sounds like you're apologizing for "having" to add affiliates when you're doing it because you want to. Don't apologize for making the choices that are right for your blog. Also, if you're adhering to the rule that you are trying to be helpful while making money, you don't need to apologize.

Keep Adding Great Content

Don't slack off on your blog's content while you play around with affiliates. Keep up the great content because regardless of what else is going on with your blog, your readers want that first and foremost. If they see you updating your blog regularly and writing great stuff, they'll roll with whatever changes you're working through on the affiliate end.

Don't Flip Flop

The best way to truly work it as an affiliate is to choose products you personally believe in. This will make you believable because you'll be telling the truth. But don't flip flop with stuff you recommend, saying how great one product is and then talking about a different one like it is the best ever. If you do change your mind, tell your readers why.

How Do You Know How to Choose the Right Affiliates?

Since every blog and every set of readers is different, no two affiliate strategies are going to be the same for every single blog. Still, you can choose the right affiliates for your blog by looking at other blogs in your niche area. See which blogs might closely mimic yours in terms of content, posting frequency, and readership. Many bloggers will talk about what has worked and not worked for them, so study their blogs and see what they recommend.

Also, listen to your readers, who may comment on your blogs about the types of products and services they like to use. This will help you choose the right affiliates to align with.

Finally, think like your reader. Are you okay with links that sell services you're interested in? What about those you don't care about? What about ad placement? Your own personal preference is probably not that much different than that of your readers, so give some thought and go slowly to determine which affiliates are right for you.

You've Tried Every Affiliate Imaginable and Nothing Seems to Work for Your Blog, Now What?

Not every blog works with affiliates, so if you feel like you've given it your best shot, feel free to try out a different income stream. Before you do, though, make sure you are:

- Getting enough traffic. The odds of making money with affiliates is better when more people see the ads. More traffic means more eyes.
- Still adding the right kind of content.
- Placing affiliate links in the areas where they will get the most action. Many affiliates have tutorials that help you with placement, graphics, and frequency. Study these before you give up on them entirely.
- Talking to other bloggers in a similar niche. What have they found that works best?

Placing Ads on Your Site

Affiliates are just one way you can make money but there are many others, like direct ad placement. This is when someone purchases space on your blog and pays you through a source like PayPal. They give you a graphic and a link where they want the ad to go, and you determine in advance how long it will stay up.

For instance, many authors place ads on my Working Writers site advertising their books when they come out. I have a variety of different ad packages that are affordable for every budget, so when someone is ready they send me the money and then we get their ad up and their book visible on my site. It's a win-win for both of us because I have targeted readers that love books and they have a book they want exposure for.

I've found that the best way to get the ball rolling with ads is to put up a graphic on your site where the ads will be placed that links to a blog post detailing what people need to do to make the ad happen. On my Working Writers blog I have a graphic I keep up where authors can click through to the post which describes:

- The duration of the ad
- What is permissible in terms of graphic size
- Which links are allowable (I let them link to a book page and author page, if different)
- How to pay (I include a PayPal button right on the post)

It's best to keep a spreadsheet of some kind so you can keep track of the ads and remove them when their time is up.

Besides writers, I used to accept ads from sites that frequently placed ads for writers. They would give me their logo or a graphic to use and I'd keep the ad up for an agreed upon amount of time.

You'll have to play around with pricing these types of ads. Conventional wisdom is that you start higher than you think would work and go down if you don't get any bites, but I like the opposite approach. I start low and keep ads affordable to get more of them. However, my audience (on my Working Writers blog at least) is comprised of people who are looking for ways to promote their products and books on a budget. Pricing too high would mean I'd turn them off.

My philosophy is to start low, get a feel for what people like about advertising on your site, and move the price up accordingly if you feel it's the right time.

Advertise Your Consulting Services

You can make money simply because you have experience that other people need, and your blog is the perfect place to do it. I used to offer consulting services on my dating blog years ago when I helped online daters craft profiles that would get attention. Not everyone is a writer, so my experience with online dating combined with my writing skills helped singles develop their profile so it showed off their true personality. This helped them attract the right people, and the rest was up to them. This service was a good income generator for me for many years.

Many industry experts offer consulting and it can be a good income source for their blog. For instance, Joel Friedlander from The Book Designer has a spot on his blog that says "Rent My Brain" (http://www.thebookdesigner.com/q-and-a-with-the-book-designer/). When you click the graphic it takes you to a page where he describes his background and experience, along with what he can do for you.

Sell Your Speaking Services

Your blog is not only the perfect place to advertise yourself as a speaker, it can also be the very source people search to find a particular expert in their area. I've received several speaking gigs from my blogs. One of them was searching for "dating expert" and my location and found me through my blog. We talked about prices and topics, and a month later I did a presentation for them. They also allowed me to sell my books so the speaking gig made additional income for my business.

To make this successful, create a dedicated page that lists your speaking services, possible topics you could give a presentation on, and possibly a video that showcases your ability. It's up to you whether or not you want to include your fee in that mix. Some people prefer to list their speaking fee so when someone contacts them they already know what to expect while others prefer to get a grasp of the scope of the lecture first. Do whatever is right for your personal business. If you're unsure, you can always say that your fees are affordable and customizable. That will let people know that you're willing to work with them on pricing.

Selling Blogs

Blogs are valuable online real estate, so it should come as no surprise that they are bought and sold every day, just like properties. People buy already established blogs for different reasons. Some like the fact that they're already set up, others like that there might be a following of readers, and others like that there are articles they can add to.

I sold a blog years ago that I had populated with content but couldn't keep up anymore due to my schedule. At that time, I needed to free up my time and felt that selling my site was a good way to do that while also get some money for bills.

There are several places to sell your blogs. I used Flippa (https://flippa.com), which puts a buyer's money in an account and holds it until the buyer and seller work out the details and make the transfer. This helps protect the buyer and seller. Flippa is a large market for blogs that are being sold, so listing there does get attention.

The online locations where you can buy and sell sites are constantly changing, so to get the most current information search "sites to sell your blogs" and see what comes up. Another option is to reach out to previous advertisers or even your competition. I've seen many blogs sold to someone with a similar site which makes sense since they probably share the same reading audience.

You'll have an easier time selling your blog if you:

- Have a niche of some sort. Your personal blog won't be of interest to a buyer.
- Have demonstrated income streams. Buyers like to know what's been working for you so they can use a similar method of making money.
- Have an established readership.
- Have a site that is easy to navigate and pleasing to the eye. Buyers know that complicated sites are hard to customize and make their own.

Flipping a blog might be something you do when you find that you don't have time, need a little extra money, or as part of your regular making money plan.

Paid Guest Posts

Most blogs accept guest posts for free, which is the standard practice, or they pay bloggers, which is even better. But some blogs flip the standard practice and charge people to place a guest post on their site. Why would you do this? It depends on your site. If you have a lot of people trying to guest post, it means you either have a site that performs well in search or you have a lot of page views. Or maybe you have readers that are fully engaged and as a result people want to have their writing seen on your site.

You might also charge companies who want to place guest posts on your site about their products. They write the post and you place it on your site. They get the benefit of a perpetual advertorial, and you get paid. It could be a win-win depending on your particular blog.

I welcome guest posts for free but one thing I don't like is when a blogger posts something on my site, then comes back again and again and asks for changes. This typically happens when there has been a change in Google algorithm and they now want to add a backlink to their site, take one away, add new links to products, etc. I can't keep up with my schedule and continually make these types of changes, so I will charge anywhere from $10-30 for a change like this.

I also post interviews for free, but found that several publicists wanted to post interviews on my site and were incredibly demanding and rude about when they ran.

I try to be accommodating but when a publicist or writer is demanding that I change my publishing schedule, I need to be compensated for my time. So now I include a paid option if someone insists on having their interview run on a certain day in order to fit in into their book tour schedule.

This isn't something I would typically do on all my sites, but for that particular one I needed to balance out the time I was spending accommodating people with the time lost on doing other work. A payment worked out well for both parties.

Promotional Guest Posts

You can also open up your blog to guest posts you write for a company. You can charge for this as an advertorial posting service, but remember, in order to make this work for your blog you should only agree to post services that you feel your readers would be interested in. On my writing site, for example, I'll post about file sharing products, ways to blog more efficiently, or products that help out the writers who typically visit my site. The posts are all labeled as promotional, which means I'm being paid to write them.

You can use a site like Izea (https://izea.com/) to help you find paid posts like this or contact companies directly. In the past I've contacted companies I used and liked and pitched my services to them. This helps me stay honest with my readers because they know that the things I'm hyping are those I actually do recommend or at least believe will work for my audience.

Ecourses

Your blog is the perfect place to promote an ecourse. A site like Course Craft (https://coursecraft.net/) can help you send out an ecourse which will be delivered directly to subscribers. You get paid and so does Course Craft.

You can actively promote your ecourse through blog posts and social media, and get feedback from readers to determine if what you're promoting is of interest. Ecourses work best with things that answer a question for people, offer a solution, or teach them something they thought was too difficult to learn but really isn't. They can be motivational, educational, or just plain inspirational. The ecourse should match the tone and subject matter of your blog.

To make things even more interesting, add pictures, video, and worksheets that can make the course interesting and unique.

Ecourses can be a good tie in with other things you're doing on your blog. For instance, if you're selling a book, is there a companion ecourse that can accompany it? If you're writing a tutorial, would it benefit people to get an in-depth option available in ecourse format?

Paid Membership Sites

Another alternative is to take your site and make it membership only, meaning that people have to pay to access it. Or, you could make certain areas for members only and off-limits to everyone else. This type of thing works well if you have premium content that you only want to offer for a certain rate. Maybe you have an active forum that you want your members to benefit from, or perhaps you have several tutorials that would be of value to your most treasured readers.

A paid site is another way to make money from ecourses. Instead of selling each course individually, you'll give everyone in your membership database access. Membership sites work well if:

- You have a lot of loyal readers who come back often. A paid site is a space where you could give them something extra in exchange for a small fee.
- You have a lot of tutorials, forum discussions, or information that is so valuable you don't want to post it for free.
- You have a good reputation and are known for offering value.

Some resources that can help you set up a membership site include Paid Membership Pro and Wish List.

Other Services You Offer

Another good reason to start up a blog is to promote your services. I interviewed a baker once who created a blog and filled it with step by step pictures that had people drooling. She then took those and put them together to create a cookbook.

Since I have such strong ties with social media, I offer writers many different options for tweeting out links and promotional material or posting about their books on my Twitter and Facebook pages. I use my blog to direct them to my Fiverr page, where some of my quick and cheap social media services are sold. Depending on your blog, your readers may be interested in the other things you do and your blog can help you promote them.

Book Sales

Writing books (either in the indie or traditional world) is a possible revenue stream all its own, but combined with your blog can help you make even more money. My blogs have always been big referrers to places like Amazon or Barnes and Noble, but I also used them to help sell certain editions of my books.

For instance, I sell signed books at my own blog because it wouldn't be possible with the paperbacks on say, Amazon, and also because then I can give the reader something extra when they request a signed copy. I sent one man an original picture I'd painted and another a print just to thank them for their sale. This helps me reward loyal readers who go to the trouble of looking up my information.

If you're traditionally published, you can post links to all the places your book is available. But Indies are the ones that really benefit from sales because they have so much control over how to promote and list their books on their own sites. Many bloggers even take several different blog posts they've written over the years and combine them into a first draft of a book. From there they work on polishing their manuscript and filling in gaps.

Blogs go very well with your own books because you can have ads for them, list them casually while talking about other things, and write about your process. Blogs and books are the perfect tie in for each other.

Pricing Work, Writing for Free, and Deciding on Your Rate

One of the hardest things when you're first starting out as a blogger is trying to figure out a fair rate to charge. I had a bit of trouble with this when I began, always negotiating myself down while talking to a potential client. Without them having to say a word, I would start off mentioning a figure and immediately interrupt myself with something like, "But if that's too much I could lower it to…" and then lowball myself. Those beginning bids were valuable lessons for me.

Now, I don't have a problem talking confidently about money but then I also know the value of my time. Being able to charge a rate that is fair but profitable will help you keep good customers and attract new ones. It also helps you feel good about the work you're doing when you know you're being paid what you're worth.

How Much Should You Charge for Blog Posts?

This is the big question, the one I get repeatedly from writers: What should I say when giving a quote for blog posts?

It depends on a few things. My general rate is $100 per blog post, but I also ask if I can do a couple months' worth of work at a time. I can't just write one post a month for someone because the time it takes me to get up to speed and learn about their business is then lost. It's better for me to establish a long-term relationship, and for that reason I usually request 2-3 months to start at a minimum.

When you're quoting a figure, you have to make sure you cover all the time you're going to put in to write and research the post and still make it competitive. Your price per hour may be less for a fun blog that doesn't take too much time to write or for one where you know you'll be making good contacts that you'll be able to use later on down the road. Maybe the site is a high profile one, and you're more interested in the publishing credit (which can be used to get other jobs down the line) than in getting a high rate.

Everyone has a different reason for blogging, so the amount you quote will have to reflect your personal values and goals. Knowing how to price a job is always beneficial, even if you decide that you'll take a lower rate for your own reasons.

Not all blogging jobs are created equal. Some you write with little research, while others require that you do interviews, find photos yourself, or only use accredited websites for information. Here are some questions to ask so you can quote out your blog posts the right way.

- What is the scope of the job?

- What's the word length for each post?

- Will I need to include a picture in the post? If yes, will you be providing a source or do I have to find these on my own?

- What is the tone of the post?

- Will I be highlighting news articles and including them in my posts? Or creating a mini-article for each post?

- Do I have to interview anyone?

- Will you need to approve or revise my posts or do they go direct?

- Is there a social networking expectation?

Each one of these elements takes time, so when your client gives you the answers to these questions, put together an estimate on how long the entire process will take you.

How Much Time Will It Take You to Write a Blog Post for This Client?

I can write fast because I've been doing this a long time, but even with that some work takes me much longer to write depending on what's involved. If you're new to blogging, the amount of time you spend on a post might be a hard thing to calculate. A good exercise is to do a few test posts that would be equal to the job you're quoting and time yourself from start to finish. I always make sure I add on a little bump in time to account for unforeseen issues that always seem to crop up with blogging, like computer problems, Internet connectivity, change in job scope, and client questions. When you figure out how long it may take you, then you can determine your rate.

How Much Do You Want to Make an Hour?

I've heard a zillion different answers to what is the "right" amount of per hour work. Bottom line? It's different for everyone. My ideal rate is $100 per blog post, but I do take gigs that pay less. When I started out, I took gigs that paid much less. I once had a sports writing job I enjoyed and did for $50 a post because I already kept up on all the news involved with the sport and could write original posts based on my own opinions.

I also took a job where I wrote posts for just $10 each, but they fulfilled my desire of $100 an hour because I could do ten in an hour. I recently took a gig for just $50 because it was for an outlet I've been trying to get into for a long time. I'm hoping I will get more work with them, and if I do on a regular basis it will be worth it because of the publishing credit and the fact that the subject matter fits my brand.

Be Careful of "Bonuses"

I've noticed a new trend in blogging the last few years, in that clients will offer you a per-post rate and then a "bonus." The bonus could be for your article hitting the front page of a social bookmarking site, a certain number of Tweets or Facebook likes, or getting traction on StumbleUpon. How do you take these into account?

The way I work it is this: I don't include these bonuses as part of my estimate. They are over and above, and if you make them, great, but if not, you don't want to plan out your budget on income that may or may not be there. A bonus is great, but it's not the main scope of the job.

Upcharges

Recently I bought a new stove. Just a plain, white, electric stove. The price was cheap enough, but when we finally completed the purchase, it was at least a couple hundred more. Why? Upcharges.

Upcharges are the little add ons that companies tack on to your purchase. Here were some of the add ons involved with our stove purchase:

- Delivery charge

- Charge for a plug (yes, that didn't even come with the stove)

- Delivery charge for a specific time (instead of an eight hour window you could pay more and narrow it down to two hours)

- Weekend delivery (an additional charge if you wanted it on a weekend, which is when most people are home)

Now, while it was annoying to pay these charges, we still did. We wanted a stove. It got me thinking about the charges we writers include for free that perhaps should be an upcharge. When I first started freelancing, I'd do the writing alone. No social media, no promotion, no looking for pictures…This was back in the old days, before the Internet exploded.

Now, however, I'm often expected to do social media, lots of promotion, getting images, interacting with readers, sending newsletters and more for my writing gigs. That's not bad, of course, but do I charge more for that work? Do you?

Think about the things you're "throwing in" as part of your fee. Do you really need to include them? Could they be an additional charge? Perhaps the photos you search for or some of the extra touches should be provided as an upcharge. While this wouldn't work for every client, there are plenty of them that would agree you should be compensated for the extra work you do.

Upcharges for Excessive Revisions

I'm not a fan of charging for revisions, mostly because I think clients sometimes struggle with getting their point across in what they want, and as a result you'll have to revise. I think revisions are part of business. But there has been a time or two when I've approached a client who was very unorganized and talked to them about charges for excessive revisions. The client agreed. They knew they had changed the scope of the project several times and cost me time.

Should this be an upcharge? I think it depends on the work and your client relationship.

Change in Scope

As long as we're talking about revisions, let's talk about a complete change in job. I've had this happen with a couple clients, one who was new and one long-time client.

The new client explained what he wanted, I gave him a bid, and as soon as we started working together he'd change the scope of the job. Every week he'd add something. Eventually, after a month, the job was very different than when I started. I talked to him about the scope of the job and he didn't want to pay anything extra, so I moved on from him.

With the older client, the scope of the job changed and that was to be expected. It's not unusual to work with a client a long time and have their needs change. So in this case, outline what you were doing when you were first hired, and what you're doing now. Show the client and ask for what you think is fair to cover the cost of the extra work. If you've built a solid relationship with your client, this should be easy to do.

Expectations

The other problem that's happened in the last couple years is that the more odds and ends writers throw into their work, the more things are expected. But should it be? I thought of this as we were charged for the plug for the stove. The plug? Seriously?

But without even a second thought, the sales guy said, Of course. You're buying the stove. Everything else is extra. Think about this the next time you price out a job. They're buying your writing ability, not social media or finding pictures or everything else.

What If You Are Paid on Page Views Alone?

As bloggers, sometimes we are paid by clients on page views alone, or how many times a post is viewed. I've been paid very often using this method, both as a bonus (where the client paid me a per-post rate and then another amount on top of it for the number of page views my posts received) and as a page view only rate.

The page view only rate is risky in my opinion, because there are many things that affect page views other than your writing ability. A Google algorithm change, a holiday weekend where Internet traffic is low, a change in public appeal for the subject matter... any of these can cause a severe jump or dip in page views. The jump is good. The dip? Not so much.

If you're getting paid on page views alone, without any other type of incentive or earnings, you are taking a risk. That doesn't necessarily mean you shouldn't take these types of jobs, but you should know that your pay is at the mercy of the Internet Gods and it can change. More than that, it will change. It may shoot up one day and go plummeting down the next. It may stay high for a while and lull you into a false sense of security about your future, and then come crashing down and stay down.

I've seen it time and time again, and experienced it as well. So why would you want to take these types of jobs?

Good Opportunities

I caution you against taking a job for "exposure," which seems to be the favorite word of people trying to hire writers for no pay. But the reality is that occasionally, it can be worth it. You have to determine if a website will open you up to new readers and will be worth your time. It might be.

Only you know if a job is totally worth your time. But here are some things to consider with a page view only pay rate:

- Is there any way you can ask the client for a post plus page view pay rate, even if you have to take a lower page view calculation. For instance, if a client offers you $1.00 per page view, could you ask for a $50 per post fee combined with a 50 cent page view bonus? Do some hard calculations before you decide.

- Is this job for a main source of my income, or as a bonus?

- Am I doing the job for other reasons (getting a publishing credit, hanging out with other writers, reaching new readers) so the page view rate is no big deal to me?

- Is this truly a viable client who will pay on time and accurately?

Asking to Be Paid When You've Been Writing for Free

Some writers start out writing for free because it's fun, they are not confident about their ability, or they're writing for a friend or acquaintance and didn't feel comfortable charging. I've been asked by bloggers many times about how you take that job you're doing for free and get some income from it.

In my opinion, you either think of yourself as a paid writer, or you don't. Don't be shy about asking to be compensated for your time. There are times when writing for free is okay. Virtual tours, guest posts, and charity fall into that.

I mentioned earlier in this book about how I started giving away articles for free in exchange for a link to my book. I looked at each article as marketing and was happy to give them to sites for free. But what if I had just asked if I could have been paid for them? What if, instead of looking at the articles as something I was doing to get exposure, I looked at them as something that built my brand?

It would have been easy for me back then to ask to be paid. Even with having a link to my book in the article, it wasn't unreasonable to ask for some compensation for an article that had the potential to stay up forever on someone's site. I didn't do that back then, but isn't it great to learn from someone else's mistakes? That's why I love sharing them.

If you've been working consistently for a magazine, newspaper, company, or organization, and you've been writing for free and they are continuing to ask you to do more articles, then it's time to change tactics.

How to Ask to Be Paid

Usually, writers start out writing for free somewhere because it's a good opportunity for them or because the client is small or a nonprofit, for example. But there comes a time when you want compensation, and I've seen many writers suddenly get upset because they aren't being paid. But you can't get angry at the client for not paying you. After all, you agreed to the arrangement.

Instead, change your focus. You're a professional writer now, and as such, you'll need to leave your old writing life behind. The right way to do this is by giving notice to your old "working for free" way of life.

For that reason, you have to be prepared to leave behind jobs you did for free. You can't say, "Hey, do you think you could pay me? No? Okay then, I'll just keep writing for free."

That doesn't work!

Instead, approach a client with a respectful tone (after all, you gained experience in writing for them – so be grateful) and let them know that you're moving on to become a paid writer. You could say something like:

"I've enjoying working with you, and hope I can continue to do it. From this point on, I am searching for paid assignments, so if you have something like that in the future, please feel free to contact me."

Then, give them proper notice, just as you would if you were leaving a regular job. If you're doing a weekly column, give them at least two weeks to a month. For a monthly post, give them at least two months' notice.

If they say they can't pay, tell them again that you've enjoyed working with them in the past, and hope you'll get the chance to do it again one day. Your point is made, there's no need to apologize for it or beg. If they can't pay you, move on to someone that can.

Counteract the Exposure Claim

Sometimes writing opportunities really are that good that they will automatically give you a boost in your exposure. If someone says they are giving you exposure, do your homework. Things you can do to help decide if it's worth it:

- See if they can give you a Google Analytics report on their traffic. Understand the difference between hits and unique visitors.

- Find out their Alexa ranking.

- Get their subscriber numbers.

- See how many Facebook likes they have.

- See how they use Twitter (not just the Twitter numbers they have.) You can have someone with a lot of followers, but if they don't use Twitter often enough they won't have the same influence as someone that uses Twitter the right way but has less followers.

- Ask if others on the staff are being paid. (That's bold. I know. But you'll surprised at what you hear. One site told a friend of mine that they did pay "certain writers." If they can pay some writers, they can pay them all.)

If someone is really paying in exposure, they can do it in more ways than just giving you a link with your article. They can help promote the article and you. See if they regularly retweet their writer's links, if they help promote in other ways, etc.

Be Ready With a Price

If you do ask to be paid for articles, you might be surprised when they agree. It happens. So before you even ask, have a reasonable idea in mind what you think you should earn, because they may ask you, "What would you like to be paid?" or "What do you think would be a reasonable fee?"

Do your homework and confidently give them a price. Don't be shy or uncertain about it.

Exposure Versus Backlinks

There is a difference between exposure for exposure's sake, and backlinks. We all write for free these days occasionally but there is usually a good reason for it, like we're promoting a book, we're blogging on a site with some writer friends, or we are trying to break into different specialties.

For instance: I write for friend's blogs for free, when I'm doing a virtual tour to promote my books, or when there is the occasional really great opportunity. In these cases, I'm guest posting to get backlinks, doing a favor for a blogger friend, or promoting my book or blog, etc.

But then there's the notion of exposure. You can consider the advantages of truly great exposure as part of your overall pricing strategy. One well-placed guest post on a high-level blog could raise your profile and help you get better rates down the line. As a rule, though if someone offers you exposure as part of your payment, be cautious and determine if this is really going to benefit you down the line.

Before you take a job writing for free, ask yourself:

- Is this an opportunity that is better (traffic-wise, pay, connections) than if I posted on my own blog?

- Will doing something for free for this person help me get other paying jobs? (In other words, is the editor really connected where they would hire you again for a paying gig down the line? Do some checking.)

- Will doing this gig establish that I'm willing to write for free. (That's a hard precedent to break.)

- Will doing this gig take too much time away from promoting myself in other ways?

Raising Your Rates

When you first start out blogging the idea that you'll have to raise your rates with someone can seem like a far off concept. But if you keep clients long enough, eventually you will have to raise your rates with them. This needs to be done right to avoid losing your client.

Is Your Client Already Paying You Fairly?

Before you raise rates, consider the work to determine if your client is really paying you fairly. If you need to raise rates because you don't have enough other work, that's not a good enough reason. If your client pays you what you should be paid, then a rate discussion isn't important.

This brings up a good point about determining your ideal rate. You need to have an understanding about what your ideal rate per hour is. This will help you when taking on new work and figuring out when it's time to boost your rate. Your ideal rate should cover your time, insurance costs, taxes, and expenses.

Justify the Rate Increase

Don't apologize for raising rates, but know that you will have to justify the rate increase with the client.

You can't just say "I'm charging more" without a good reason, or your client may leave. Instead, give consideration to how much you need to make and what kind of increase is reasonable. When determining rate, look at:

- How much time it takes you to write a post (letter, press release, or whatever piece you generally work on).

- If you need to do research, determine the time it takes you to find sources and gather information.

- If you need pictures, factor in costs for you to buy pictures, find the right ones, credit them, etc.

- If you need to promote your writing, factor in costs for social networking and marketing.

- Factor in your costs for taxes and insurance.

If you do all this and come to the conclusion that your client is not paying you correctly, you now know what the new rates should be.

Approach Your Client

Before you approach your client about the rate increase, practice justifying it out loud a few times. I've found that the best way to do this is either on the phone or in person. Of course, a lot of this depends on your client. If you have one that prefers only email or text communication, you'll have to do it that way.

Arm yourself with the knowledge of what the rate is now, why you're raising it, and what it will be going forward. When you decide to raise rates you aren't asking a client's permission to do it, so be prepared if they balk or say no. No one wants to volunteer to have their rates raised, so it's natural to get some pushback. Allow the client some time to "sit" with this information, but don't back down or apologize.

When you make the decision to raise rates, you are doing it because you want to keep the client and your costs need to justify doing that. Don't sound timid or embarrassed about having to raise your rates. If you need to do it, do! It's for your business.

Some things I've said in the past when having this conversation with clients:

"When we first started working together my rate was X, but after three years the scope of the project has increased. I'm now interviewing sources and gathering personal data before I can write

the posts, and this adds considerable time to the research process. I will need to raise my rate to X to continue."

"I enjoy working with you and hope I will be able to continue. I've taken a look at the rate I'm charging you and found that it isn't in line with other clients similar to you, so I will have to raise your rate a bit so I can keep my schedule open for your work."

"Since my deadlines are tight I will need to raise your rates to X in order to accommodate the quick turnaround projects we've enjoyed working on together."

Learning From Plumbers on Setting Freelance Rates

I like to look at other industries when it comes to things like rates and see what I can learn about my writing business. Just because I'm a writer doesn't mean my business model is all that different from say, a plumber's. I still have emergencies to tend to, regular clients, and the need to put food on the table for my family.

A few years ago our garbage disposal went on the fritz so we picked one up from the local home store. To install it, we hired a plumber. Here's some things I learned about rates from that visit.

An Emergency on Your Part Doesn't Mean an Emergency on Our Part

Just because your faucet is leaking all over the floor doesn't mean it's the plumber's problem! They might come running right away, but they will charge you appropriately. If you need a plumber during off hours or a rush job, you'll pay more.

Compare this to what freelance writers do. I know that in the past I've done a rush job for someone and didn't charge extra. I thought at the time that I was getting a new client, but in many cases that client used me for one rush (and usually, difficult) job and then never called me again. I should have at least asked to be compensated for:

a quick turnaround, doing work on weekends, or coming in to fix something another writer did.

Peace of Mind in a Job Done Right

One reason we decided to hire a plumber to install our disposal is that we have an older house and weren't sure we could install it properly. We called a plumber because we knew that if he did it wrong, he would come back out and fix it. We got a guarantee and peace of mind from him.

Compare this to freelance writers. So often businesses think "anyone can write" and assign various writing tasks to project managers, assistants, and marketing people. But are these people the best for the job? Will someone have to go back in and update the work they did? Freelancers need to do a better job about guaranteeing their work. Give them peace of mind that when they hire us, we'll come back and fix things if it isn't done right and they won't need to worry.

No Apologies for Rates

Our plumber was here a total of 12 minutes (yes, I did time him), and he charged $95. The time included a trip charge and his time. Despite that this was an easy job for him, he made sure his time was compensated and didn't apologize about the cost.

Compare this to freelance writers, who are sometimes afraid to give a quote for fear that it will be too high. Have you ever given your rate and felt the need to apologize or explain? Why should you have to do that? Your rate is your rate. No apologies.

Trip Charge

Let's talk about that trip charge. Plumbers tack on a cost just for the plumber to get in his truck and come out to take a look at your plumbing issue. If he doesn't do anything else, he still gets paid to come out and visit you.

Compare that to freelancers, who often spend time meeting with clients outside the office. You might drive a long way or spend a great deal of time away from your writing talking about a project, but will you ask to be compensated for this?

One reason I started doing so much online writing is that I didn't like client meetings. Some clients couldn't get used to a writer working from home and as a result needed to "see" my progress. Rather than assure them that my time was better spend working on their project than driving in to show them what I was working on, I continued to drive in to their office, spend money on gas, and waste time in meetings that I didn't need to be in. If I had charged a trip fee to them, this might have been different. At the very least, more of my time would have been compensated.

How Much Do Bloggers Really Get Paid?

Learning about what other bloggers make can give you inspiration on what you can potentially earn. Or, it can depress you, depending on what you hope to gain and the type of person you are. I like to see what the most successful people in my business are up to so I have inspiration on tips and techniques I can apply for my own blog. I also like to see what's possible.

As you make your way in the blogging world, I can tell you that it is very possible to make a good side living or full-time income, but you have to treat it as a job. I feel as if I'm always pulled in different directions, and yet, I wouldn't trade this job for anything.

Here's some helpful links that will encourage you to keep after your blogging for money dream.

- Carol Tice talks about making $5,000 a month blogging:
  http://www.makealivingwriting.com/how-i-make-5k-blogging/

- Amy Lynn Andrews have a very helpful post about how much bloggers really make:
  http://amylynnandrews.com/how-much-do-real-bloggers-actually-make/

- Several bloggers share their monthly income figures at Work at Home Resources and Advice: http://wahadventures.com/2013/06/bloggers-share-income.html

- Income Diary has the top earning blogs: http://www.incomediary.com/top-earning-blogs

Maintaining Your Blog Business

So now you've set up your business and maybe even made some money. How do you keep the blog business going? In my decade of blogging I've seen the industry change many times, and that's part of the challenge. Search engines change, people change the way they read and look for information on the web, and trends change. You'll also deal with some burnout. That's the downside of blogging.

The upside is that you'll be meeting amazingly creative people, getting recognition, expressing your creative thoughts, and developing a platform. It will be a wild ride but worth it.

Avoiding Burnout

I know, everyone talks about burnout and it seems like it applies to every industry. The very nature of blogging means that you're online, writing, and pouring energy into your business all the time. If that sounds tiring, maybe it isn't the job for you. Most bloggers have experienced burnout but have learned how to cope while still refusing to give up.

My biggest deterrent to burnout is keeping a schedule I can manage. I like to schedule ahead as much as I can to keep from that "oh no, I need to come up with a post" mentality that leaves some writers scrambling. I also like to take breaks if I need to. I'll go for a walk, get up and take the dog out, or just take a nap if I need to. You can't come up with fresh ideas if you're tired.

I also like to blog from different locations when I'm feeling tired and cranky. I'll take the laptop to the coffee shop or the park to remind myself that having the freedom to work from anywhere is really a huge bonus.

What About Social Media?

Blogging goes hand in hand with social media, but the combination of the two can be a little overwhelming. I like to use social media to promote my posts and also to get ideas, find out what people are curious about, and interact with readers.

Social media has become essential today for writers to build a platform and get your work out there. But getting the most out of it and working it correctly is a challenge for some writers. I see a lot of people trying to "sell" rather than interact, and social media just doesn't work this way. You can promote your stuff but you need to do it in the right way.

Be a Person First

Remember the first word in social media: social! Always be a person first and a marketer last. In between "first" and "last" are all the things that tell readers about who you are. In other words, don't start off by sharing links about your books or blogs. Instead, start off by connecting with readers and getting in on the conversation.

Some of the writers who do social media well have large followings because readers enjoy their personalities. They interact with writers and then (and only then) look for what else that writer does. This is the right way to do social, because it allows people to discover you on their own, and then buy your books and spend money on your blog in their own time.

Follow Some of the Folks Who Do It Right

You can learn a lot about how authors are using social by how some of them are using it. Here's some of my faves from Twitter and Instagram:

On Twitter:

- Neil Gaiman: https://twitter.com/@neilhimself
- Margaret Atwood: https://twitter.com/MargaretAtwood/
- Judy Blume: https://twitter.com/judyblume (Her Twitter bio alone shows you how clever she is. It says, "Are you there, Twitter? It's me, Judy.")

On Instagram:

I so love Instagram and hope you'll join me on there (https://instagram.com/cherieburbach). I think Instagram offers a way to show people about your world without the clutter of Facebook. I like it as a complement to Twitter.

Here's some of my favorite Ingrammers:

- Amy Tan: https://instagram.com/amytanwriter

- Jon Krakauer: https://instagram.com/krakauernotwriting/ (The scenery alone will draw you in, and that's the point.)
- And Stephen King: https://instagram.com/stephenking, of course, for pictures like this: https://instagram.com/p/f5xxHglkAk/.

Get Creative

One of the coolest things I saw was how Philippa Gregory actually tweeted out the entire thoughts of her character Elizabeth Woodville for her historical fiction novel *The White Queen*. Gregory took her perspective from the book and boiled it down into individual 140 character tweets for the whole novel.

Then, after the book launched, she put all the tweets in an application that you can **read again and again**: http://www.philippagregory.com/thewhitequeen/twitter/.

Hang Out Where Your Readers Are Hanging Out

One reason Jennifer Weiner (https://twitter.com/jenniferweiner) has such a successful Twitter following is that she live tweets during her favorite TV shows like *The Bachelor*. Why? Because that's where her fans are! (Plus, she really likes the show.) She also answers her fans there and comments on celebrity gossip and things going on in her household. This works for her and her genre. Know what she doesn't do? Send out endless links about her books!

Share Some Parts of Your Life

You don't have to get all TMI on the world, but go ahead and share some things about yourself that people might find interesting. I post a lot of pictures of my dog because she's here with me as a write all day and quite frankly, she makes me laugh. I also post about various things I'm thinking or I try to be encouraging.

Since you're sharing, you'll need to choose which parts of your life you'll share and which you'll keep private. There is a way to be on social media and share certain things without giving away the private moments of your life.

Be Genuine

We've all seen writers who feel obligated to do Twitter or Facebook because someone (their agent, publisher, or another author) told them they need to be on it. As a result, their efforts seem forced and inauthentic.

Never go into social with half the effort because you'll be wasting your time and turning off readers. The best thing you can do is to embrace social (at least one platform), get comfortable in it, be yourself, own it, and enjoy it. If you don't, skip it and find another way.

Some kind of social media presence is essential when you're a blogger. Twitter is my number one source of non-search engine traffic, so if you use it correctly you can not only promote your blog but also grow your followers.

How Much Social Influence Do You Have?

Part of the challenge in relaying what your platform really is involves numbers. It's not just the Twitter or Facebook numbers you have but the way you use social networking. Someone with 3,000 Twitter followers can actually have more influence than someone with ten times that amount simply because they know how to engage properly.

Social influence is important because without it you'll have a shaky platform. That means that you might have the "numbers" that make it look like you've got the platform, but as soon as that platform is used it will fall apart (meaning: you won't sell books or ecourses, no one will visit your blog, and there will be no engagement with readers.)

Here are some ways to help determine your social influence. It should be noted that even these are things you need to take with a grain of salt. It's best to use a combination of sources and information to really determine the answer to how far your "social reach" really goes. Never rely on just one thing.

Klout

Klout tries to determine your social influence by a combination of things including Twitter, Facebook, Linked In, etc., and even things like Wikipedia. (Seriously.) It measures not just followers but how many times there is engagement (someone responds to you, retweets you, etc.)

The scores go from 1-100, the higher your score the more "influential" you are. Average Klout scores are about 40, and anyone with a 63 or above is in the top 5% of all users.

Kred

Kred seems to build on the concept of influence by adding "outreach." So with Kred, you have two different scores.

The first score relates to your influence. This works similar to the Klout score: when people like your content, share it, respond to it, your score goes up. Anything about 700 is considered a good Kred influence score.

The second part of the score is outreach, which determines how likely someone is to share, retweet, or comment on your stuff. The score goes from 1-12, with seven or higher being "an impressive score."

Twitter

Twitter is very misleading because people think it's all about numbers, which it isn't. They also think you sit there and look at the Tweets that come in and that's how you connect on there. It isn't that either.

It's a microblogging platform that allows you to search for keywords, make lists of people (even if you don't follow them) and easily see what's trending. Someone with a million users may tweet out something once a day that is never seen by their users while someone else with 2,000 users will have had good conversations with people and really make their influence known.

To see if someone is influential on Twitter, check out the number of people that respond to them, the variety in the tweets they share (comments, links, and random thoughts) and how often they use the site. Someone that tweets out an automatic link once a day isn't very influential.

On Your Blog

Blogging is still a great way to determine your influence. How many people come to your site? How many stay? How many are new users and how many are return visitors? This will tell you if they are "one and done" visitors or loyal.

Also, check your **Alexa Rank** (http://www.alexa.com/) and **Google Page Rank**. Both are important for their own reasons. If Alexa, for example, says they don't have enough data to look at your site, you've got some beefing up to do.

Feedback From Readers

Hearing from readers involves more than just blog comments or tweets. If readers seek you out, send you emails, and tell you they enjoy your work, this is huge. People are busy and don't have time to just look up someone and read their articles or books. If they do, that's a great thing and a good indicator or your influence.

Twitter Is a Great Option for Bloggers

Of all the social media outlets, I'd say Twitter matches most perfectly with blogging. I've found it easy to use, a good way to research information for blogs, get opinions, and find out what's trending. Pairing the right blog post with a trending hashtag, for instance, can help your blog traffic soar. This helps you with client work and for your own blogs.

Twitter is perfect for interacting with your readers, because not only will they chat with you, they will also:

- Give feedback on your books and blog posts (with links to their reviews)

- Provide a place for you to test out ideas about things (think online focus group)

- Help promote your books and blog posts (by tweeting and retweeting links)

Twitter also gives readers one more place to find you. Tweets are indexed by search engines, so when a reader searches your name or your blog, Twitter gives you one more place where you can be found, which strengthens your brand and makes it easier for people to find you and your work.

Also, bloggers are generally very supportive of each other. That's one of the great things about writing online. You can use Twitter to help promote other bloggers. Pointing your readers to other blogs they may enjoy makes you look that much better to them, and will help you connect with writers who may do the same for you down the line.

Besides all that, I find that Twitter doesn't become a time suck for me like Facebook does. I don't know about you, but when I get on Facebook, I end up spending way more time than I would otherwise want to spend. There are games, people's photos, and much more to distract me on Facebook. I don't have that issue with Twitter. While you still need to interact with people on Twitter, the time you spend on it is much less than other forms of social media.

Using Twitter to Get Blog Post Ideas

When I'm trying to get a few ideas for some blog posts (or when I want to see what people are saying about certain subjects) I use the Twitter search function. Pop in a term in the search bar and see what comes up. This will not only help you be more social on twitter but also give you a wealth of ideas. You'll find out what's buzzing, what people are blogging about, and what their questions are. Twitter is a good communication tool, so use it to ask readers what they most want to learn about or what their opinions are.

Interviews

Twitter is also a good place to find sources. In the past I've sent out a request for certain subject experts and someone sent me the name of another person, and when I followed up with them I was able to secure an interview. In this case, Twitter works almost as if you're all in a giant office together and you're walking up to the water cooler in order to find out what's going on.

Trending Topics

The trending topics feature will help you keep abreast of the news and also tell you what people are talking about most. If folks are talking about it, maybe you should blog about it. Connecting to a trending hashtag can boost your page views, and starting a hashtag can help you keep organized or develop a series.

For example, if you have weekly post about blue dresses, you could use #BlueDresses or #colorinfashion as you tweet out the link. Then you can easily refer back to it or use it as a way for readers to add their own comments.

Interview Someone on Twitter

I've been interviewed on Twitter many times. A few months ago I did a Twitter chat for the **BBC** talking about ex-pats making friends in America (http://www.bbcamerica.com/mind-the-gap/2014/10/09/mindthechat-qa-friendship-expert-cherie-burbach/).

The chat was fun and a way to connect with people from all over the country. During the chat I answered questions, tweeted out links, and interacted in a really fun way. Later, I was able to link to some of the individual tweets and hashtags to promote the blog posts I mentioned during the chat.

5 Things to Do Daily to Quickly Promote on Twitter

Most of the complaints I hear from authors about Twitter is that it's time consuming or difficult to use. Neither is true, but when you're already pressed for time, adding one more method of promotion can be the straw that broke the camel's back. But not this time! Here are five quick and easy things to make Twitter work for you.

1. Automatic Tweeting

Automatic tweeting can help save you time. You should still interact on the site, but in order for your tweets to be seen by the most people possible, you need to send them more than once. There are several great sites that will let you do this. Here are a couple:

- Twuffer
- Networked Blogs
- Buffer

What I do is spend several minutes one or two times a week scheduling various tweets with links that I feel need the most attention. These links could be related to book reviews, guest posts, or information on your blog. Once you set them up, you don't need to think about them again.

2. Be Present on Twitter

By "being present" what I mean is get active. Again, this doesn't take much time. But if the only effort you're putting into Twitter is that you tweet something out once or twice a day and that's it, step it up. A good rule of thumb? Interact with five people and tweet out five things. Do that to start, and see how you do. How you do find people to interact with? Read on.

3. Use Twitter Search

That search box at the top of Twitter is your friend. Use it to find people who are:

- Chatting about your subject area.
- Talking about a news item that might relate to our blog.
- Promoting books or blogs similar to yours.

Finding people to interact with is a key component of Twitter. You can't just tweet out links and be done. Not just that, but finding people on Twitter is easy. Enter a search term in the box, see what people are saying, and get involved in the conversation. It doesn't take long.

I use Twitter a lot for non-writerly things, but it still connects me with potential readers. I tweet about TV shows, music, my dog, and a variety of other things going on and it's always an interesting (if short!) conversation.

4. Promote Other Bloggers

I mentioned this briefly above, but promoting others is a great thing to do. Not only is it polite and gives you a "plays nice in the sandbox" kind of vibe, but you'll also help your readers find new writers. Isn't it nice when an author or blogger you enjoy points out other stuff you might like? That helps you with your own readers, and it also helps you find new readers. If you promote an author who is similar to you, they might do the same for you.

5. Inspire People

Who doesn't love an inspirational quote or saying? You can be the person that gives someone a lift. The great thing is, when you inspire someone else they will probably follow you, so spread out your tweets with promotional items and things that provide inspiration.

Another way to do this is to find other writers and give them an "atta boy." Writing is such a solitary thing, so it's nice to be heard when you talk about your WIP. Search for the #amwriting hashtag to find out what writers are working on, and respond to them with a note of encouragement.

These quick five things will keep you in front of the eyes of Twitters everywhere, and get you more attention and success when using Twitter. Use these tips to slowly build a Twitter platform where you naturally talk about your blog as well as other things that might interest in the Twitterverse.

How to Keep Your Blog From Getting Boring

Did you ever find a cool writer and follow them to their blog only to find out that it's boring? So disappointing. How can a writer who knows how to draw you into a story or article leave you wanting when it comes to their blog? Depending on your attitude, blogs can become boring if your heart isn't in them. Or if you're busy. But you need to keep it fresh or readers won't come back.

The fact is, blogging is about moments in time and it's not always going to be perfect. So let go of that "perfection" goal because it doesn't exist. Instead, just be you. People aren't perfect, but they are interesting and flawed. That's why we like them. We like when they take us into their world and just show us who they are. Blogging contains our personalities and thoughts. That's why we love reading blogs so much. It's us, even at our ugliest. Even when we're feeling broken. Even when we're so happy we don't know what we're saying.

Blogging is the culmination of our words, all our growth, our changing attitudes, and the thoughts that never change. Blogging takes all these small moments in time and puts them together, so you can get a sense of who we are.

When You're So Sick Of Your Blog You Could Just Hit Delete

There might be a time when you actually get really sick of your blog. When you just can't stand the thought of writing one more post. When that happens, here are some things to try:

Take a Break From It

I know the conventional wisdom is that you should blog regularly and never take a break. Or, that you should announce you're taking a break, prepare for that break with guest posts, and then come back exactly when you said you would.

The problem with this approach is that it doesn't take into account those times when you're sick to death of your blog. When you're at that point, step back. Call it a break or call it blog preservation, but mentally and physically take a break.

I've done that with every one of my blogs at some point. After years and years and daily posts, I got burned out. I took a break for a few months, and when I did I had a new appreciation for my blog all over again.

Change the Template

You know how a new haircut can totally change your perspective? A new template can do that for your blog. A new template can help you clean up code and give your blog a completely fresh look. This alone can motivate you to keep it up.

Re-Evaluate Your Reasons for Blogging

If your passion for blogging has changed, maybe your reasons for blogging have changed also. If you were once the expert in X but aren't anymore, naturally you're not going to want to blog about it. This doesn't mean you need to stop, but maybe you need to change your approach. Perhaps you'll now except guest posts and get another perspective, or change the type of posts you write. Take a step back and read through your old posts as you figure out where you stand with the topic now.

Surf With the Purpose of Getting Inspiration

Nothing inspires like other bloggers. The blogging world changes quickly, so see what else is happening in the blogosphere and it may inspire you to change some things on your own site. I like seeing which trends are hot in blogging and how those might apply to me.

What's Your Real Blogging Voice?

Blogging is different than other forms of writing in that it is meant to capture your own unique voice. A reader going through your blog should feel as if they are sitting down with you over a cup of coffee. You can be reflective, serious, or funny, but you need to be natural.

I've read blogs from people I know that don't sound like them at all. As a result, I feel disappointed that I'm not getting a sense of their personality. So don't worry about how you "should" sound on your blog. Don't try to be funny if you're really not, and don't try and copy anyone else. Just be you.

Blog About Your Hobbies

What do you do when you're not writing? Share that on your blog. Show pictures about the things you do in your free time and talk about the hobbies that interest you.

Your Struggles

No one expects writers to be perfect. In fact, they're usually better when they're not. What about your background? Your current struggles? Include some of these in your blog. You don't need to get too personal if you're not comfortable with it, but you can share a few things that will make you more relatable to someone else.

The Story Behind the Story, But Make It Interesting

I've seen writers talk about "their process" in such a way as to bore readers to death. Don't try to make it more complicated than it is, but do share what prompted you to write a story. Make it about something the readers would be interested in.

Your Guilty Pleasures

Am I the only one that watches Real Housewives? No, I'm not, and when I blog about those types of things, I always get responses. That's because we all have a few guilty pleasures, and if you can share them your readers will be able to relate to you on a whole different level.

Your Joys

Sharing "your joys" is different than bragging about your life. When you share the things that bring you joy, you're bringing readers into your world. When you brag, you're putting them off.

Staying Motivated

Freelance writing and blogging is something that can be difficult to get into initially, and even harder to maintain an income with. It is filled with rejections and uncertainty. Even the most experienced of freelancers can get frustrated by the continual search for work and dealing with objections.

Writers typically work alone, so having other likeminded people around to understand and support you is an important part of succeeding as a blogger. If you're not able to hang out with writers face-to-face, an online forum can work just as well. A search for "writers" on Facebook can help you find groups that can also lend support.

The key to being successful in a writer's group or forum is to listen and provide support for others. The more genuine a friend you are to other writers, the more support you will receive in return. This is something that can't be faked, so take some time to get to know your fellow writers in order to reap the benefits of their understanding and advice.

Who Is Your Virtual Cube Mate?

Recently I got some really good news about an article I did, and I wanted to share it with someone. But then, I'm working at home. Sometimes I go to a coffee shop, but even then I wouldn't have just waltzed up to a stranger and said "Hey, guess what just happened to me!"

But lucky for me, I have a few people I can call when I need a human (a real human, not just a Twitter or Facebook human) connection, and I called up another writer friend who lives across the country, but who I've chatted with numerous times. We like to encourage each other. I shared my news with her, and she said, "Wow, so I'm your virtual cube mate?" What a cute way to look at it.

I think it's extremely important to have people you can call up and also see face-to-face when you're a writer. Never underestimate how important a human connection is. A lot of bloggers, especially when you're working full-time, are very isolated. We're also people who enjoy spending time by ourselves, but we need to break that up with real people now and then. It is one thing to post something on Facebook and get a "great job" or "like" but another entirely to hear the voice of a friend tell us they are happy for us.

Mutual clients or writing sites are a great way to find virtual cube mates. Here are some others:

- Writers groups
- Meetup groups (your cube mate doesn't have to be another writer)
- Friends from old jobs (from before you were a writer)
- Others who are at home during the day (shift workers or stay at home parents)

- Church

Of course, being a virtual cube mate means you have to be a friend, too. So make the most of your relationship by reciprocating the goodwill. So be available for your virtual cube mate, offer cheer, and most importantly, listen. See how this type of relationship can make you a more complete person and better blogger.

Staying Current on Trends

Blogging has changed a lot in the last few years and will continue to change. It's important to stay on top of current trends and what's happening in our industry. I love reading the **SEO Moz blog, Mashable, Mind Tools**, and **Search Engine Land** for things about blogging, digital trends, and SEO. I read a ton of lifestyle sites to keep up on which types of articles are most popular, ways to write blog post titles, and how articles are presented online.

It's important to know what's really happening with the online world so you can keep current, but at the same time, stay true to yourself and what you most want to accomplish by blogging. You might want to change your blog template from time to time but you don't need to. You might want to do whatever is the latest trend with your titles or ads but you don't need to. All you need to do is what's right for you personally. Always have your goals in mind when writing and don't feel the need to compete. Your blog's success isn't dependent on anyone else, and your success might look entirely different than someone else's.

Blogging Resources

Many of these resources were listed in the book but I've gathered them here as a handy reference. Some of these are affiliate links, which means if you purchase something I may get some money from it. I have the links broken out by function.

Things on the web change very quickly and I will try very hard to keep them updated, but if you find out a link is incorrect before I do, I'd appreciate you letting me know. Feel free to contact me: http://cherieburbach.com/contact/.

When Setting Up a Blog

Become a Blogger: http://www.becomeablogger.com/resources/ (I used this site as a reference to set up my own series of WordPress blogs).

Michael Hyatt's guide to setting up a WordPress blog in just 20 minutes: http://michaelhyatt.com/ez-wordpress-setup.html.

Entrepreneur's Journey (a very helpful site for many reasons) offers tips on how to start a blog from scratch:

http://www.entrepreneurs-journey.com/7698/how-to-start-a-blog-from-scratch/.

Mashable's how to set up a WordPress site: http://mashable.com/2013/06/11/wordpress-how-to/

StudioPress: http://www.studiopress.com/ (the site I use for templates). I've used them to set up several blogs over the years and their stuff makes my sites look professional for very little cost and effort.

Helpful WordPress Plugins

- Woo Commerce: https://wordpress.org/plugins/woocommerce/
- Contact Form 7: https://wordpress.org/plugins/contact-form-7/
- Google Analytics by Yoast: https://yoast.com/wordpress/plugins/google-analytics/
- Image Widget plugin: https://wordpress.org/plugins/image-widget/
- Instagram Slider Widget: https://wordpress.org/plugins/instagram-slider-widget/
- WordPress Popular Posts: https://wordpress.org/plugins/wordpress-popular-posts/
- Simple Social Icons: https://wordpress.org/plugins/simple-social-icons/

- Author Avatars List:
  https://wordpress.org/plugins/author-avatars/

Photo Resources

- Morguefile: http://www.morguefile.com/
- Canva: https://www.canva.com/
- Picmonkey: http://www.picmonkey.com/
- How to Use Getty:
  http://www.pcworld.com/article/2105163/how-to-use-gettys-vast-collection-of-newly-free-pictures-on-your-website.html

SEO

- Search Engine Land:
  http://searchengineland.com/library/google/google-panda-update has background on the Panda update.
- A comparison between Panda and Penguin:
  http://seoupdates.info/difference-between-google-panda-and-google-penguin/ from SEO Updates.
- The "winners and losers" of the Panda update:
  http://blog.searchmetrics.com/us/2014/09/26/panda-update-4-1-winners-losers-google-u-s/

- Jeff Goins' non-robot approach to writing: http://goinswriter.com/choosing-seo-keywords/
- Copyblogger approach to SEO writing: http://www.copyblogger.com/seo-copywriting/

Job Boards

- Freelance Job Openings: http://www.freelancejobopenings.com/
- Online Writing Jobs: http://www.freelancewriting.com/freelancejobs/onlinewritingjobs.php
- Problogger: http://jobs.problogger.net/
- Blogger Jobs: http://www.bloggerjobs.biz/category/blogger-jobs/
- Whisper Jobs: http://ed2010.com/whisper-jobs/
- Dice: http://www.dice.com/
- Journalism Jobs: http://www.journalismjobs.com/index.php
- Media Bistro: http://www.mediabistro.com/joblistings/
- All Indie Writers: http://allindiewriters.com/freelance-writing-jobs/
- Indeed: http://www.indeed.com/

Staying Up on Current News

- SEO Moz blog: http://moz.com/blog
- Mashable: http://mashable.com/
- Mind Tools: http://www.mindtools.com/blog/

Thanks for Reading!

I'm very excited that you decided to become a blogger in some fashion, either full or part time.

I wish you much success to you in your writing journey! If you enjoyed this book, please let others know!

Blessings,

Cherie

About the Author

Cherie Burbach is a freelance writer specializing in lifestyle and relationships. She's written for About.com, NBC/Universal, Match.com, Philips Lifeline, and more.

Whether it's writing about caregiving, finding love, or making new friends, all of Cherie's fiction and nonfiction centers around relationships and faith.

Cherie's poetry reflects the faith and hope that is evident in her life story. Cherie also likes to express herself with mixed media art, combining Bible verses and her own poetry with special papers and acrylics. You can see some of her works at **her** Etsy shop: https://www.etsy.com/shop/CherieBurbach.

For more on Cherie, visit her website: http://cherieburbach.com/.

www.ingramcontent.com/pod-product-compliance
Lightning Source LLC
Chambersburg PA
CBHW070926210326
41520CB00021B/6819